Praise for *The Art of Work*

"*The Art of Work* will make you think differently about what you do and how you do it. Jeff Goins is a fresh young voice in a field full of copycats. He challenges us to approach our work the way we would a canvas—both delicately and with furious discipline. People will be reading this book, and profiting from it, for a long time."

—STEVEN PRESSFIELD, BEST-SELLING
AUTHOR OF *THE WAR OF ART*

"This is one of the most honest, direct, and generous books about you and your life that you will read this year. It took guts to write and it will take guts to read. Leap."

—SETH GODIN, BEST-SELLING AUTHOR
OF *WHAT TO DO WHEN IT'S YOUR TURN*

"Today, unlike any previous time in history, we have options about the work we do and the role it plays in our lives. But it is precisely here that so many of us get stuck. With so many choices, we struggle to figure out what we really want or where to start once we do. In *The Art of Work*, Jeff Goins provides a clear framework for discerning our calling, developing our mastery, and maximizing our impact. This is the plan we've been waiting for—from a guide we can trust."

—MICHAEL HYATT, *NEW YORK TIMES*
BEST-SELLING AUTHOR AND FORMER
CEO OF THOMAS NELSON PUBLISHERS

"This is the real stuff. *The Art of Work* is a powerful dive into what matters, how to connect with that inside yourself, and then how to bring it out into the world in a useful way. This book will push some buttons you want pushed, and from there, it will guide you toward a new level. Dig in."

—CHRIS BROGAN, *NEW YORK TIMES*
BEST-SELLING AUTHOR OF *THE
FREAKS SHALL INHERIT THE EARTH*

"'Every story of success is, in fact, a story of community.' Lines like that and the powerful truth behind them are why I'm such a big fan of the books Jeff Goins writes. At times, *The Art of Work* felt like I was reading my diary. Jeff has such a knack for clearly articulating the thoughts we've all quietly wondered!"

—Jon Acuff, *New York Times* best-selling author of *Do Over* and *Start*

"How would it feel to go to work each day because you wanted to—not because you had to? In *The Art of Work*, Jeff Goins shows you how. This is a real-life treasure map that can lead you to the life you were meant to live."

—Chris Guillebeau, *New York Times* best-selling author of *The Happiness of Pursuit* and *The $100 Startup*

"I used to think hating your job was just a normal part of every adult's life—that is until I discovered I could build a job I actually loved. Thank goodness for Jeff and thank goodness for this book. Here's to not waiting one more day to find, build, and engage in work you love!"

—Allison Vesterfelt, author of *Packing Light* and founder of yourwritingvoice.com

"If there were just one chapter I could recommend to my colleagues and clients from this book, it would be 'The Portfolio Life.' Just *this*! I won't spoil it, but I *will* say it gave me a permission to *be* and embrace what I suspected about myself (and apologized for) for my entire life! I'm living a portfolio life, and you can't make me go back to conventional wisdom. Thanks, Jeff— this book is a must-read for the creative spirit, the restless soul, and the lifelong learner anxious to make things happen!"

—Carrie Wilkerson, author of *The Barefoot Executive*, carriewilkerson.com

"Jeff Goins takes away the mystery of discovering and mastering your true calling, all with a healthy slice of reality thrown in. Thoroughly life inspiring."

—CHRIS DUCKER,
AUTHOR OF *VIRTUAL FREEDOM*

"Our hearts crave connection to a meaningful calling. *The Art of Work* shares the process for hearing that calling and then doing the work that feels like 'slipping into an old pair of shoes.' A must-read for anyone wanting to live a life that matters—fully alive."

—DAN MILLER, *NEW YORK
TIMES* BEST-SELLING AUTHOR OF
48 DAYS TO THE WORK YOU LOVE

"*The Art of Work* accomplishes the next to impossible, providing clear, relevant, useful guidance on finding your calling while being enormously enjoyable to read. It is required reading for anyone who is asking, 'What should I do with my life?'"

—PAMELA SLIM,
AUTHOR OF *BODY OF WORK*

"*The Art of Work* is encouraging, uplifting, and meaningful. I cannot recommend it enough. It may be one of the best books on finding your purpose in life I've ever read. If you've ever wondered what your life should be about, this is a book you should pick up and read today."

—JOSHUA BECKER, *WALL STREET JOURNAL*
BEST-SELLING AUTHOR OF *SIMPLIFY*

"No more excuses! *The Art of Work* illuminates the path for anyone who wants to embrace their calling and build a body of work they can be proud of."

—TODD HENRY,
AUTHOR OF *DIE EMPTY*

Reader Reviews

"*The Art of Work* is a practical, yet inspiring prescription for how to identify and nurture your true passions in life, allowing you to turn a calling into your own beautiful contribution to the world. It's full of stories of regular people who have come alive by following their vocations and overcoming the greatest obstacle: fear. Jeff's writing has forever changed my outlook on chasing my dreams."

—Jennifer

"I have some simple criteria for enjoying and defining a book as good: I don't want it to end. I could and will re-read the book. It touches my heart, and I know it will touch the hearts of others. *The Art of Work* met all those criteria."

—Bryan

"If you're feeling stuck in life, read this book. In it, Jeff gently prods you to rethink the idea of a 'calling' while encouraging you to recognize that you already have one. Then he gives you practical steps to start identifying what that calling is, which might just help to unstick you."

—Brandi

"*The Art of Work* is chock full of inspiration that will motivate you to live your best life. Jeff's encouragement to 'just take the next step' is a roadmap that will have you going from overwhelmed to accomplished. Looking to live life on your terms? Permission granted!"

—Kimi

The Art of Work

A PROVEN PATH *to* DISCOVERING WHAT YOU WERE MEANT TO DO

JEFF GOINS

NELSON
BOOKS

An Imprint of Thomas Nelson

Published in Nashville, Tennessee, by Nelson Books, an imprint of Thomas Nelson. Nelson Books and Thomas Nelson are registered trademarks of HarperCollins Christian Publishing, Inc.

Published in association with The Youth Cartel, 8511 Victory Road, La Mesa, California 91942.

Interior designed by Mallory Perkins.

Thomas Nelson, Inc., titles may be purchased in bulk for educational, business, fund-raising, or sales promotional use. For information, please e-mail SpecialMarkets@ThomasNelson.com.

Unless otherwise noted, Scripture quotations are taken from THE NEW KING JAMES VERSION. © 1982 by Thomas Nelson, Inc. Used by permission. All rights reserved.

Library of Congress Cataloging-in-Publication Data

Goins, Jeff.
  The art of work : a proven path to discovering what you were meant to do / Jeff Goins.
    pages cm
  ISBN 978-0-7180-2207-5 (paperback)
  1. Vocation. 2. Vocational guidance. 3. Self-realization. I. Goins, Jeff. II. Title.
  BL629.G65 2015
  331.702--dc23

2014023732

Printed in the United States of America

15 16 17 18 19 RRD 6 5 4 3 2

For my siblings: Nikki, Marissa, and Patrick.
May you make your mark on the world.

Contents

Author's Note

What's happened to you is rare," my friend Mark said to me just before I made one of the most important decisions of my life—the decision to quit my job and become a full-time writer. My last day at work also happened to be my thirtieth birthday, which made it a milestone in many respects. The truth, though, is the day itself was less significant than the process it took to get there.

When asked how I got to this point, I struggle to give an intelligent answer. The experience of finding your calling can be both mysterious and practical. It takes effort but also seems to happen *to* you at times. What I've come to understand is that finding your purpose is more of a path than a plan: it involves twists and turns that you never expected. Ultimately these surprises lead you to your destiny. And once you arrive at what you thought was the destination, you realize it's only another leg in the journey.

This book is a description of that path, as well as the steps it takes to navigate it.

Everyone, it seems, is searching for a purpose, for something to satisfy their deepest desires. I believe that "something" is a calling.

What is a calling? You will hear me use the word interchangeably with the terms *vocation* and *life's work*, but quite simply, it is the reason you were born.

When I began working on this project, I thought I knew what the process of pursuing a dream looked like, but what I found surprised me. Discovering your calling, it turns out, isn't quite so simple. The journey looks different for each person, but there are common themes that consistently emerge. If we look at those themes, we can identify a pattern that will help us understand our own vocations a little better.

What if what happened to me wasn't so rare? What if everyone has a calling? That was the question that sent me on my journey. The people whose stories appear in this book, many of whom I personally interviewed, are not extraordinary, in the sense that you've heard their stories before. They are not typical case studies for success, and that was intentional. In these seemingly ordinary accounts, I think we understand our own stories, which often feel far too ordinary for our liking, a little better. Some readers might be disappointed with the subjectivity of such a book. But this is the way we live our lives—not as research projects and book reports—but as anecdotes and emotions. And in each experience, we find certain truths we might otherwise miss. My hope is these stories connect with you in ways that plain facts cannot, and in reading them, you too are changed.

The Art of Work was not the book I intended to write but ended up being the one I was supposed to write. A calling is like that too, I suppose. It is the thing that you never thought would be, the twist in the plot that makes everything else come together, and somehow in the end you cannot imagine otherwise. Writing this book illuminated my own understanding of how purpose and vocation work together, and I hope it does the same for you.

Introduction

The Cancer That Couldn't Stop a Triathlete

Many are called, but few are chosen.

—MATTHEW 22:14

A calling is not some carefully crafted plan. It's what's left when the plan goes horribly wrong.

One June evening in 2000, Eric Miller skipped a company meeting to watch his five-year-old son play T-ball. During the game, he and his wife Nancy noticed their little Garrett was having problems placing the ball on the tee and couldn't seem to balance properly. Concerned, they took him to the doctor, who immediately ordered a CT scan. When the Millers were asked to wait in what medical professionals call "the quiet room," Eric knew something was wrong. As a nurse, he was well acquainted with the purpose of that room. It was where people went to receive bad, sometimes horrible, news. The time was six in the evening.[1]

By 11:30, Garrett was admitted to Children's Hospital in Denver, Colorado, and immediately sent into surgery. The next morning, on June 24, a golf-ball-sized tumor was removed from the back of the five-year-old boy's head. He was diagnosed with a *medulloblastoma*—a word, his dad says, no child should ever have to know.[2] After the surgery, Garrett was left blind, mute, and paralyzed. Put on a ventilator to help him breathe, he would have to learn how to walk, talk, and go to the bathroom all over again. Even if by some miracle he was able to do all that, he was still given only a 50 percent chance of surviving the next five years.

The Millers began counting the days they had left with their son.

One day in the middle of the cancer treatments, while looking at his son, Eric thought about how the clock was running out on Garrett's life. In spite of the challenges facing his little boy, and the worry this caused, he realized something. It was an epiphany of sorts. Working in the medical profession, an industry "where the clock runs out on people all the time," Eric realized he was wrong. It wasn't just Garrett's life that could end at any second—it was all of theirs. There was no guarantee *anyone* in the Miller family would outlive Garrett.

"We needed to be living life *all* of the time," Eric told me. "Because none of us are guaranteed that we're going to be around an hour or two from now." Whatever time they had left, the Millers were going to live life to the fullest.

After Garrett was moved out of the ICU and taken off the ventilator, his dad wondered if there was anyone out there who knew how he was feeling. Sitting in a window bay of the hospital, he prayed for an answer to the despair that threatened to destroy what little hope his family had left.[3] That was around the time he discovered the story of Matt King, an IBM engineer and world-renowned tandem cyclist who happened to be blind.[4]

That fall, Eric took his son to meet Matt King at a nearby cycling event, where Garrett got the chance to sit on a tandem bicycle and squeeze the handlebar with his hands, feeling the pedals beneath his feet. That was the day the "light bulb" came on for Garrett. After that, he was determined to ride again—which, unbeknownst to him or his dad, was the beginning of a process that would not only change their lives but the lives of countless others.

A few months later, Garrett told his mom he wanted to try riding his bike. She wasn't so sure, but he insisted. By then some of his sight had returned, and he was able to walk, albeit just a little. With his mother's help, Garrett mounted the old bike and began pedaling. At first she ran with him as he pedaled clumsily, helping him balance. But soon his legs took him faster than she could run, and he escaped her grasp, if only for a moment to experience the freedom he had known before the cancer had taken control of his body. That same day, his dad brought home a brand-new tandem bicycle so the two of them could ride together.

Six months later, on June 24, 2001, after a year of radiation and chemotherapy, six-year-old Garrett crossed the finish line of his first-ever triathlon. His dad ran behind him, pushing his wheelchair. It was one year to the day after that first debilitating surgery.[5] For the father-and-son duo that had endured so much, the race was a way of declaring to the world and perhaps to themselves that they would not let one little tumor stop them from continuing with their lives, from celebrating life itself. Thanks to the clinical treatments his parents had enrolled him in, Garrett's survival rate had now increased to 90 percent.

That was fourteen years ago.

Since that first surgery that nearly crippled him so many years ago, Garrett has competed with his father in more than a dozen triathlons, as well as one on his own. His eyesight, though not fully restored, has returned to the point that he can see blurry objects and shapes. He is still considered legally blind but can do things the doctors said were impossible. He is, without exaggeration, a walking miracle.

—⁓—

This is not a book about miracles. It is a book about finding your calling, about how you discover what you were born to do. A calling is that thing that you can't *not* do, an answer to the age-old question, "What should I do with my life?"

There are books that talk about how to find your dream job or what it takes to become an expert—this just isn't one of them. *The Art of Work* is a book about *vocation*, a word that has come to mean something very different from the original definition. The word *vocation* comes from the Latin root *vocare*, which means "to call." It was originally used in a religious sense, as in a call to the priesthood. And for centuries, people thought of it as just that— something reserved for an elite group of people, for those special few who were lucky enough to be called.

But what if that isn't true? What if a calling is something *everyone* has?

In this book, I will try to recapture that ancient understanding of vocation as something more than a job. Through stories of everyday people, I will argue that much of what we think about calling, if we think about it at all, is wrong. The way to meaningful work doesn't always look like a carefully crafted plan. Sometimes the route to our purpose is a chaotic experience, and how we *respond* matters more than *what* happens to us.

Each chapter tells a different person's story, illustrating a major concept—one of seven stages of a calling. And although the stories differ, they all share one similarity: each person was in some way surprised by what he or she found. This, I think, is a story we don't hear enough of today—one that just might help us understand our own personal journeys better. And where do we see this more than in the story of a five-year-old boy who beat brain cancer and went on to race in a triathlon?

In his eighteen years of life, Garrett Rush-Miller has completed a half Ironman, climbed Machu Picchu, and earned the rank of Eagle Scout. When he's not at school or working at the local climbing gym, he spends his free time volunteering with Wounded Warriors, a charity that supports and encourages war veterans. At the time of this writing, he's getting ready to graduate high school and more than anything would like a girlfriend.

After Eric e-mailed me with some news clippings of his son's story, I immediately picked up the phone and called them. Speaking with both of them during Garrett's lunch break, I was struck by how positive they were and how important perspective was in their story. Theirs wasn't a rags-to-riches tale or some super-spiritual experience. It was inspiring but also quite practical. All they were doing was trying to survive, making sense of life along the way, and *that* was a story I could relate to.

I asked Garrett if he ever thought about what life would have been like if he had never missed the tee that day, if he had never gotten the brain tumor and hadn't had to go through sixty-four weeks of chemo.

"I've never really thought about it, to be honest," he admitted.

His dad said the same. "The reality," Eric explained, "is these are the cards we've been dealt, and we'll just play them the best we can."

Eric Miller has always tried to steer his son in the direction of what he *can* do, not what he can't. And that little lesson has led to some incredible experiences for both of them. The gift that Garrett's dad gave him wasn't protection from pain or suffering, as much as Eric would have liked to provide such things. It was helping Garrett see that what makes a life extraordinary aren't the chances we get, but what we do with them.[6]

Course Correction for Your Calling

At some point, you entertained the idea that you were born to do something significant. But then high school happened. Or college. And your parents talked you into becoming a lawyer instead of a baker. That professor told you med school was a smarter move than relocating to New York to try out an acting career. And you believed them. When "real life" began, you gave up, but called it growing up instead and abandoned the dream altogether. You made excuses for why wanting something extraordinary was somehow selfish and immature, and you wondered if any of those youthful feelings were ever real in the first place.

But even then, you knew you were wrong. No matter how noisy the world got, no matter how busy you became, there would always be something inside you—a small voice that whispered in the quieter moments of life, taunting you with the shadow of the unlived life. If you listen hard enough, you can still hear it.

Everywhere you look, people are giving excuses for not pursuing what they were born to do. Some say they are "a work in progress," while others shrug with indifference, saying they're still trying to figure out what they want to be when they grow up. Such phrases sound harmless, but they are anything but. If we're honest, a lot of us feel stuck, aimlessly wandering from one job to the next, unsure of what to look for or even expect. We've accepted our lot in life. *It is what it is.* Even though we do our best to embrace reality, we are restless. What comfort do we have other than the vague notion that we're not alone?

As we enter a new era in human history, as the average lifespan increases and the world becomes an even more efficient place full of technological solutions, people are asking deeper questions. We now realize the way we've been doing work no longer works. Factories are getting smaller, not bigger. The forty-year career is dead. The world demands a fresh approach to vocation, and we need something new—or perhaps, something very old.

There is a way to meaningful work that doesn't force you to conform to your parents' career path or to compromise your values. It won't be like any class you've taken and probably won't resemble what your teachers told you the future would look like, but it can be trusted. There's more to life than what happens to you and more to a vocation than punching a clock.

But how do we find such a way that seems so far gone?

The journey described in this book is an ancient path. It's the way of master craftsmen and artisans, a centuries-old road that requires both perseverance and dedication—the narrow path that few find. Here we follow in the footsteps of computer scientists and park rangers, participating in the same process that made world-famous cartoonists, compassionate missionaries, and successful entrepreneurs.

At times you will have to trust your gut, and at others you will need to do what is uncomfortable and even painful. But as you go, there will be signs along the way, markers ensuring that you are headed in the right direction.

The path described here is not a manual for life. It's a piece of canvas on which to add your own experience. This isn't some science experiment with predictable results, and it won't be another self-help program that leaves you feeling passively inspired.

After encountering hundreds of stories from people who found their calling, I've identified seven common characteristics, each illustrated in the subsequent chapters. Each chapter, which tells at least one person's story, is based on a theme:

1. Awareness
2. Apprenticeship
3. Practice
4. Discovery
5. Profession
6. Mastery
7. Legacy

You might want to think of these as steps, but they are more like overlapping stages that, once begun, continue for the rest of your life.

For example, once you learn the discipline of awareness, you continue to practice this throughout your apprenticeship, continually looking for guidance along the way. The same is true for practice—it's something you keep doing long after you acquire a skill.

There *is* a process to finding your life's work. Although at first it may feel chaotic, there is an order emerging from such chaos. And if you commit to following these stages, paying attention along the way and persevering, you will have something rare, something you can be proud of.

Letting Go of What Could Have Been

"Part of people's problem is they think of everything that could've been," Eric Miller told me after his son left our phone conversation. "Who *cares* what the future might've been for Garrett? It doesn't matter. It can't be. This is where we're at, and this is where we're going."

In his voice, I could hear the military stoicism that must've served him well while dealing with more than a decade of raising a special needs child, not to mention during his career as a paramedic and nurse. He went on to tell me about his subsequent divorce and confessed that pining for what could have been only holds people back from living their lives now. Life is full of surprises, and it doesn't help us to fixate on regrets or try to recover what has been lost.

"Maybe . . . that's a lot of people's problems," he added, "is they keep thinking, *what would've happened if . . . ?* Who gives a crap? It just happened."

But what would *not* have happened if Garrett had never gotten sick?

"Now that's a whole different question," he admitted, his tone softening. "We think about that all the time. *None* of this would have happened. My life would be totally different."

None of this. Not the triathlons, not the foundation they started, not the countless lives affected—none of it would have happened had it not been for a tragedy that struck the Miller family fifteen years ago. Because of Garrett's illness, Eric is now able to encourage others in a way that would have been impossible before. Working in an intensive care unit at a hospital, he gets to speak with suffering people all the time.

"I have authority now, because of Garrett's suffering," he said.

What hope does he offer these patients? What encouragement does his pain provide? He tells them to hold their heads high, even when they don't think they can.

"More people are watching your life and . . . are gaining strength in their own lives and in their own challenges because of what you're going through. I promise you: your life matters, your life is significant, and things are happening that you don't even fully understand yourself."

That's what Eric has done and what he's encouraged his son to do: To acknowledge that whatever is happening in their lives now, as difficult as it might be, is important. To not hold out for the right opportunity or wait for things to get better, but to make the most of life now. The question that Garrett Rush-Miller's life answers is the same one many of us are afraid to ask: *What happens when the life you end up living doesn't look like the one you planned?*

Each of us has had surprises and setbacks in life, disappointments that have disrupted what we *thought* was the way. And we're left with something that looks less like a personal purpose and more like a mess. Hearing Garrett tell his story, I wondered if the difference between remarkable people and the rest of us has little to do with circumstance and more to do with mindset. Maybe we all have the power to turn our lives into significant stories if we start to see our difficulties as opportunities.

We can't control what life throws our way, but we can control how we react to it. As we do, maybe we come closer to a meaningful life than any plan could ever take us. To do this, though, we have to let go of what we think we deserve and embrace what is, which just might lead to something better than we ever could have imagined.

Your life, though not an accident, is full of surprises. The point of this book is to help you know what to do when they come.

PART ONE

Preparation

ONE

Listening to Your Life

The Call to Something Old, Not New

Before I can tell my life what I want to do with
it, I must listen to my life telling me who I am.

—PARKER PALMER

You don't "just know" what your calling is. You must listen for clues along the way, discovering what your life can tell you. Awareness comes with practice.

The halls of Emory Hospital were particularly busy that day as Jody Noland navigated the crowds to locate her friend's room. She brushed past people visiting their loved ones, and a queasy thought came to her: *How could something so terrible be happening to Larry?*

Larry Elliott had recently decided to reprioritize his life, selling his successful insurance business to serve hurting children in the world. It began with serving alongside his wife, Bev, as house-parents at a children's home in Alabama but had led to a leadership position at another children's home outside of Atlanta. He was changing gears in what he thought would be the second half of his life, but he had much less time than he realized.

Larry and Bev decided to take their family on a long-awaited vacation to Europe. This was a chance to spend some quality time together and reconnect with their kids. It was a trip everyone was looking forward to.

The pain started on the flight to Italy, beginning with a throbbing sensation between Larry's temples. In Florence, a CAT scan revealed a mass in his brain, and the family was forced to end the vacation prematurely. On the flight home, the pilot had to fly at a lower altitude to minimize the amount of pressure in Larry's head. The next morning, he was scheduled to go into surgery. At forty-eight years old, Larry was battling a brain tumor.

His room wasn't that difficult to find, as Jody later recalled in her book: "It was the one where people overflowed into the hallway."[1] There was not enough space to fit all the friends he had accumulated in his lifetime. And in spite of the pain, Larry did his best to comfort his visitors.

There was a sense of urgency to his demeanor that day. At one point, he asked his wife if she'd brought a pen and paper, something that seemed odd to Jody. Later she asked Bev what that was about, and Bev explained that Larry wanted to write a letter to each of their children before going into surgery. He didn't know if he would make it out alive and wanted to express his love, affirming what was so unique and special about each of his children.

Larry lived another nine months before ultimately losing his life to cancer.

That same year, Jody lost two other friends who were both in their forties and passed away without warning. The deaths came as a shock to everyone. As Jody watched three grieving families, she thought of the comfort Larry's words had provided his family. She hurt for the children, those "who knew unquestionably of their parents' love, but desperately missed the reassurance and security that their physical presence provided." She couldn't stop thinking of the letter he wrote and the difference it had made.

Jody started sharing Larry's story with others. "Don't you think this is something we should all do for the people we love?" she would say, trying to drum up interest. And many would respond, "Yes, but I'm not a writer," or, "Yes, but I have no idea where to begin."

"One way of knowing our gifting," Jody told me, "is when something that seems easy to us doesn't seem easy to others. I kept thinking, *How hard could it be?* Maybe I could help people do this . . . What seemed so hard for so many people seemed easy to me."[2]

She eventually relented to that prompting.

Jody established Leave Nothing Unsaid, a program and book that helps people of all ages write letters to their loved ones. After Larry's death, she had been inspired, but the idea didn't become reality until she decided to act. She kept thinking someone should do something. Finally she realized that someone was *her*.

At fifty-eight years old, Jody Noland is beginning to understand how her life has been converging for decades on this very moment. She is doing what she was born to do, and although the circumstances have been hard, even painful, she's learned an important lesson. All along, her life was teaching her something, even in the pain. And if she hadn't paid attention, she just might have missed it.

Happiness Is Overrated

There are two stories we hear when it comes to pursuing a dream. First is the tale of the self-made man or woman. In this story, we see a driven individual overcoming adversity and defying the odds to achieve success. Many of us have believed this is the *only* way to achieve anything—through sheer tenacity. The process is simple: set a goal, work hard, and achieve your objectives. You can be anything you want, do anything you want; all you have to do is work hard. You are in complete control of your destiny. But things are not always so simple.

In the film *The Secret of My Success*, Michael J. Fox plays a young upstart named Brantley who is trying to get ahead in the corporate world. After continual rejection, he finally explodes in another failed job interview, saying: "Everywhere I've been today there's always been something wrong: too young, too old, too short, too tall. Whatever the exception is, I can fix it. I can be older; I can be taller; I can be anything."[3]

Like many people, Brantley believed that if he put his mind to it, he could accomplish anything. In the end, though, he realized the secret of success is that sometimes getting everything you want doesn't always make you happy.

The second story is the opposite of the first. Instead of the self-made path, you have a determined one. Whatever will be, will be. Life happens in spite of what we want. You have no control over anything, and in the end, you will look back on your life and understand there could have been no other way. But where is the adventure in that—in having everything scripted out for you? And what of the countless stories of those on their deathbeds, confessing regret? Even when we talk in terms of "destiny" and "fate," we want to believe we have some control over our lives. There must be another way.

The first path says you can be whatever you want; the second says you have no choice. But perhaps there is a third way. What if there was more to your purpose than getting what you wanted? What if there were some things you couldn't control, but how you reacted to those situations made a difference? *Is* there a purpose to your life, or are we all just bouncing around in a chaotic universe? Everyone from religious scholars to scientists and career counselors has pondered these questions. So let's look at them pragmatically.

Here's what we know. A lot of people are unhappy with their jobs, where they spend a significant amount of time. A recent poll found that only 13 percent of the world's workers are "engaged" in their jobs. The other 87 percent feel disconnected from work and more frustrated than fulfilled.[4] These numbers shouldn't come as a surprise. When a friend says she hates her job or a family member talks badly about his boss, we aren't shocked. This is acceptable behavior. We've been conditioned to think of work as drudgery, a chore you endure in exchange for a paycheck. And this is a problem.

When you are stuck fulfilling an obligation instead of chasing a dream, you aren't your best self. We all know that. This is why we find more and more people moving from one occupation to the next. They are doing their best to be happy but failing miserably. Most of us have done this at some point, quitting one thing for the promise of something better. And we were disappointed to find that the next job or relationship held the same complications as the one we were escaping.

But maybe we're going about this all wrong. Maybe the worst way to be happy is to try to be happy. The work of acclaimed Austrian psychiatrist Viktor Frankl supports this idea. A Holocaust survivor, Frankl had intimate experience with suffering, and it taught him an important lesson. Human beings, he argued, are not hardwired for seeking pleasure and avoiding pain. They want meaning. In spite of what we say, we don't want happiness. It's simply not enough to satisfy our deepest longings. We are looking for something more, something transcendent—a *reason* to be happy.[5]

As part of his life-saving therapy with suicidal patients and his own experience in a Nazi concentration camp, Frankl learned there are three things that give meaning to life: first, a project; second, a significant relationship; and third, a redemptive view of suffering. He realized that if people, even in the bleakest of circumstances, have a job to do, something to return to tomorrow, then they have a reason to live another day. For Frankl, the book manuscript he had been working on before entering the camp and the hope of seeing his wife were what kept him alive. And in time, he was able to see the purpose in his pain. Because he had work to do, someone whom he believed was waiting for him, and a certain attitude toward suffering, he survived it when others did not. And his memoir, *Man's Search for Meaning*, became one of the most popular books of the twentieth century, affecting millions of lives.[6]

What we often don't realize is that making our story about us, even about our pain, is the wrong approach. Dwelling on the past or fixating on the future won't help you find fulfillment. The way you beat a feeling of purposelessness, according to Frankl, isn't to focus on the problem. It's to find a better distraction. Which is a roundabout way of saying you have to stop trying to be happy. But doesn't everyone want to be happy? Maybe not. Life is too short to do what doesn't matter, to waste your time on things that don't amount to much. What we all want is to know our time on earth has meant something. We can distract ourselves with pleasure for only so long before beginning to wonder what the point is. This means if we want true satisfaction, we have to rise above the pettiness of our own desires and do what is required of us. A calling comes when we embrace the pain, not avoid it.

Tragedies, unfortunately, are inevitable. Bad things happen to good people, whether we want them to or not. What determines our destiny, though, is not how successful we are at dodging hardship but what we do when it comes. Pain and suffering, though intimidating obstacles, are not strong enough to keep us from our purpose. In fact, they can sometimes be the very catalysts for such discoveries.

That's the lesson Jody Noland learned from her friend Larry and what she almost forgot when her own husband was on his deathbed.

The Good Kind of Fear

Fear is a powerful deterrent, but it can also be an effective motivator. The fear of failure or rejection can be unhealthy and irrational, but fear of not telling your loved ones how much you care is important. So not all fear is bad. Some people, though, let fear run their lives. They avoid risk, hoping to minimize the chances of failure, and in effect move in the opposite direction of a calling. The trick is to know when to listen to your fear and when to not.

In 2009, Mike Noland, Jody's husband, was diagnosed with stage four liver cancer. Jody started searching the Internet for what she could learn about his prognosis. Realizing he had little time left to live, she began to prepare for the inevitable. Mike, however, had other ideas.

His way of coping was to deny the imminence of death. In Jody's words, he "hunkered down" and refused to acknowledge reality. He didn't read about his condition, didn't ask the doctors any questions, and continued with life as usual—except, of course, for the regular chemotherapy and radiation treatments.

"In the midst of all of that," she told me, "he was concerned about his clients and whether it was time to execute a buy-sell agreement on his business. Doing that meant he was accepting his certain death sentence. The day the agreement was executed, his mind began to fog."

Listening to Jody relate the story over the phone years after the fact, I could still hear the pain in her voice. I could feel the urgency. She pleaded with Mike to write letters to his children, a gesture she had seen make a dramatic impact in Larry's family. In fact, so moved by her friend's gesture, she had begun helping others do the same by teaching a letter-writing workshop that empowered people to share words of affirmation with their loved ones. She wanted her family to receive that same comfort she had provided for strangers. But her husband resisted. He didn't believe the cancer was that serious. And after weeks of trying to persuade him, even resorting to writing the letters *for* him, Jody finally gave up, deciding to comfort her husband with whatever time they had left.

The cancer killed Mike quickly. Within three months of the

diagnosis, he was gone, never having started a single letter. After the funeral, his daughter Nancy asked Jody if he had written any letters like the ones her stepmom had helped others write. Jody was devastated. She felt like a failure. In spite of her encouragement and occasional nagging, none of it had worked. She knew the power of letter writing, the impact a few words of encouragement could make. But there were no letters for Nancy, no words of affirmation from her now deceased father, and there never would be.

After Mike's death, Jody wondered whether or not she should continue the letter-writing workshops.

"My immediate conclusion was that I should abandon this dream," she recalled in her book. "How could I advise others to do this when I had failed so miserably in my own home?" She doubted if this was something she was called to, after all. "I really thought I had misunderstood."

Jody gave away the workbooks she had made, keeping only one as a keepsake, and she let the grieving begin.

A year later, a man called her, looking for a copy of the workbooks she used to have. His wife's best friend was dying of breast cancer and wanted to write a letter to her two daughters. She was desperate but didn't know where to begin or what to say. Jody explained she wasn't doing the workshops anymore but sent the woman her one remaining workbook. "Her death was so imminent," she wrote, "that a courier was sent to pick up the workbook."

Several weeks later, Jody received a thank-you note. Because her workbook had helped the dying mother express her love for her daughters in writing, she was able to spend the last few weeks of her life in peace. Jody wept. All this time, she had been afraid of failing, of trying and not succeeding, but now she understood what was really at stake. She knew the thing she had to fear the most was failing to answer this calling she had received, no matter how much it hurt.

"I would rather go for it and fail than not try," she said.

What We Learn from Fairy Tales

At the beginning of every story, we see something that looks a lot like normal life. Long before the protagonist slays a dragon or embarks on a quest, we see her in some unsuspecting place, dreaming of something more. In *Beauty and the Beast* (my personal favorite Disney classic), Belle sings of wanting more than "this provincial life." In *Star Wars*, Luke can't wait to escape the boredom of a farmer's life. And in *The Wizard of Oz*, Dorothy sings about life "somewhere over the rainbow." Our lives are haunted by the ghosts of what might have been.

It's easy to dismiss such people as dreamers or even downright crazy. But are they really? Before a chain of events sets the hero on course to his destiny, there is a sense that there should be more to life than *this*. You may be feeling it right now. At an important moment, everything makes sense, as it did for Eric Miller when he realized the clock wasn't ticking away on his son's life any faster than his own and when Jody Noland saw how significant a letter from a loved one could be. This is what storytellers call the "inciting incident," the moment when everything changes and the tale of an average person living an average life becomes one of mythic proportions.

But something must occur for this to take place. The person must enter the story, either by choice or because she's forced into it. Belle goes to find her father. Luke leaves home with Obi-Wan. Dorothy gets swept up in a tornado. In any great narrative, there is a moment when a character must decide to become more than a bystander. It's an important moment that always seems to happen in the mind before it unfolds in real life. This choice, though, is always preceded by something deeper, a nagging feeling that there must be more.

This is why when people are called to some great task, they know it. Immediately they recognize the prompting to step up and do something significant, because they have been waiting for it. Before the call comes, we must possess some sense that awakens us to our purpose.

Awareness, then, is what prepares us for the call.

Before you know what your calling is, you must believe you are called to *something*. It doesn't matter if you know what. In order to cultivate awareness, you must be willing to act, to step out and see what happens. And once you are convinced that purpose will not find you, that you will have to go in search of it, you are ready. Until you make this choice, though, you will feel frustrated, seeing people succeed and chalking it up to luck or some unfair advantage. And in doing this, you will deceive yourself.

The truth is some people do get lucky, and others have been born into special privilege, but what are those things to you? You are still called.

A calling may be many things, but it is not fair. Still, you must answer it.

Before you begin your life's work, you need to prepare. Chances come to us all, but only those who are ready recognize them. You don't need some big plan. You just need to be a little dissatisfied. You need to have some vague premonition that the world is not completely right. That's what *awareness* is: a sense that something more is possible.

You don't need a lucky break or a golden opportunity; you don't even need to "just know." What you do need is the desire and willingness to begin. Only then can you dedicate yourself to the work that is required of you, and only then will you know what it's worth. Without awareness, you won't be able to recognize the opportunities that come. And they always come to those with open eyes.

The Wrong Kind of Fear

I don't have a dream. It was the fear that haunted my thoughts that day, lingering in my mind. I sank down deep in my seat, surrounded by a hundred pairs of hopeful eyes. We were all there, gathered in that multipurpose room (which was doubling as a conference center that day), for the same reason. To pursue a dream. To find the thing our hearts had been searching for.

Some of us wanted to be novelists; others aspired to start our own ad agencies or travel to South America to make a documentary. Each dreamer represented a unique and beautiful dream, some special skill the world needed. The passion in that room was infectious, which only reinforced the feeling that I did not deserve to be there.

"What's your dream?" was the opening obligatory question, and we all did our best to respond in kind. It was even something we had to inscribe on our name tags. I think mine said something profound and nondescript like "creative catalyst." In other words, I didn't know.

I had no idea what my dream was or what I was doing there. When people asked what I wanted to do with my life, I used big, fancy words and complicated phrases that meant little to me but caused people's eyes to glaze over just enough so that they were too intimidated to ask any follow-up questions. Which was precisely my intent.

"I want to be a storytelling sherpa," I told a guy carrying around an iPad.

He nodded, the fear of following up obvious in his eyes. Mission accomplished.

A few times during the conference, I talked about my day job, but that felt boring and unoriginal. I was sure my dream was something new and interesting, something "out there" that I'd never done before but would recognize as soon as it appeared on the horizon. At some point during the conference, it would walk up to me and say hello, greeting me with a smile, and we would start the rest of my life together.

Every time I answered another question, I felt like I was betraying myself, that people were slowly seeing through the facade and beginning to feel sorry for me. Me, the hapless wanderer who was at a dream conference and didn't have a dream. The guy with no vision for the future, just a fancy name tag. And then, just as I was getting ready to excuse myself from my table and sneak out the back exit, the opening speaker stepped up to the podium. With a few short words, he shattered my illusion.

"Some of you here don't know what your dream is," he said. "In fact, most of you don't."

I looked around to see dozens of heads nodding slowly in unison. Apprehensively, I did the same, a little worried who was watching me but eventually letting go and feeling the freedom that came with admitting I didn't know what I was doing.

"But the truth is," he continued, "you *do* know what your dream is . . . You're just afraid to admit it."

My heart sank. As soon as he spoke those words, one word popped into my mind: *writer.*

Now I was no longer afraid of failing. I was afraid of not trying.

—⚭—

What if you don't know what you're supposed to do? What if you have no idea what your passion is? These are the questions we ask when trying to figure out what we should do with our lives. And they are good questions—I've asked them myself—but they are not the right questions. When we say we don't know what to do, what we're really doing is asking something deeper. What we want to know is this: "Can you promise me I won't fail?"

And the answer is *no.* Of course not. Nobody can promise that.

Most people waste the best years of their life waiting for an adventure to come to them instead of going out and finding one. They succumb to the status quo and dream of life being different *someday.* Plagued with indecision, they wait, unsure of the right path to follow. And as they wait, they miss an opportunity to live. The only smart choice is to move, to not hold out for a better time and choose a direction now. Yes, you *could* fail, but we all know what happens when you don't try—nothing. Certainly there will be bumps in the road, even wrong turns, but at least you will be moving.

We often think of a calling as something that comes to us, an epiphany that arrives when we least expect it. But the truth is, in some ways, it's already come. You already have some sense of what you're supposed to do with your life, even if you aren't sure what it is. The trick is to find your vocation hidden in your life. That's what I learned the moment I started thinking of myself as a writer. I went looking for answers and found that some of them were already in me.

We all want to "just know" what we're supposed to do with our lives, for our purpose to be spelled out for us, but that's not how a calling works. It's never clear and hardly ever obvious, especially when you're starting out. But when you start to take those first steps, when you commit to some course of action, you begin to see what was there all along.

Most of us have some sneaking suspicion that there must be more to life than *this*. We understand we each have a part to play in a bigger story. Even if we aren't sure what that is, we know there's *something*. Those "lucky" few who find their callings testify to this. They knew there was a purpose out there, and they were determined to find it. The way that they did this was by taking the first step, by overcoming the myth that "you just know" and deciding to act anyway. And they learned, as you might, an important lesson: clarity comes with action.

At a certain point, you must acknowledge this nudge, the hint of a whisper that says life has been holding out on you. We all have some understanding of what we're supposed to do with our lives. We may not realize it or perhaps we lost it, but it's there, waiting to be uncovered. What we need, then, is not a map, but a shovel—a set of tools to start digging. I used to think a calling was something you just knew you had, and if you didn't know then you weren't called. But I've come to understand that's not the case at all. A calling is what you have when you look back at your life and make sense of what it's been trying to teach you all along.

What would you do if you could do anything? Everyone has an answer to that question. You might spend all day with the kids or travel the world or finally write that book. You might dedicate some serious time to a business idea or perhaps with the right resources buy a new camera to take photos all day at the park. Or maybe you'd just sit back and sip coffee on the porch with your spouse, embracing all the little things in life. If you pry hard enough, everyone has an answer to this question—and that's an important clue.

The problem is so few of our lives look anything like what we want them to be. What prevents us from living the life we long for is fear. We fear the unknown and what we might lose—our security, our reputation, our lives. This is what keeps us from our life's work and what numbs our awareness to the call—mystery. We are afraid of what we don't know. But the truth is you will never have clarity. As Mother Teresa once said, you will only ever have trust.[7] Fear, indecision, not knowing—these are the obstacles that keep you from moving forward. And they never go away. But if you are going to find what you were meant to do, you will have to act anyway.

What I am trying to say here is that a calling takes work. Finding yours will require a fear-facing journey that will last a lifetime. And where does it begin? With awareness. With discovering what your life is already saying to you. And as you attempt to uncover this mystery, consider one more question, a much more constructive one: What happens if you *don't* do this? That's what should really scare you.

Your Life Is Speaking

Many people wander through life, unaware of their purpose, blindly following the whims of the world. To them, those who reach their potential seem to possess an extraordinary gift. But what if pursuing your calling wasn't a luxury reserved for the elite? What if it was required to live life, fully alive? Where would you start?

Listen to your life. That's Frederick Buechner's advice. An author who spent part of his life as a schoolteacher and another part as a minister, he observed that finding your vocation is less about grand moments of discovery and more about a habit of awareness. "See it for the fathomless mystery it is," he wrote. "In the boredom and pain of it no less than in the excitement and gladness: touch, taste, smell your way to the holy and hidden heart of it because in the last analysis all moments are key moments . . ."[8] What Buechner was saying is that awareness doesn't just happen; it must be cultivated.

If you pay attention to your life and the lessons it can teach you, you won't feel so lost. Your story will seem less like a series of disjointed events and more like a beautifully complex narrative unfolding before you. You will understand each setback, inconvenience, and frustration as something more than what it appears to be. And perhaps, as you listen to it, your life will speak.

It may call to you in the early morning or late at night and tell you what you are meant to do with your gifts, your passions, and your abilities. This voice might help you make sense of what has happened to you, and it may even give you guidance. Or it might unravel a whole new thread or theme you never before considered. The point isn't necessarily what the voice says. That's important, of course, but it's beyond your control. The point is to listen.

In a world full of distractions, this is what we are inclined *not* to do. We would rather buy a book, sign up for a seminar, or attend a conference to instruct us. Take this step. Follow that program. Adhere to these six principles. But such experiences are poor substitutes for the "fathomless mystery" of life, as Buechner put it. We have been raised to believe that anything is possible, that our potential is unlimited, and that we are entitled to our dreams. But maybe finding your calling is not quite so simple.

We all want to begin with ability, with what we can do. But when have you ever been a good judge of what you're capable of? People are always doing things that amaze themselves. A calling goes beyond your abilities and calls into question your potential. And when the journey is complete, even you are surprised. Just because you *can* become an astronaut or a newspaper deliveryman does not mean you *should*. Each person is responsible to not only do what she is capable of but also what she is meant to do. In the words of author and activist Parker Palmer, don't just tell your life what you want to do with it; listen to what it wants to do with you.[3]

Here's how it works, practically. Look at the major events in your life and write them down on a piece of paper. Note everything significant you can remember, even the things that seem silly or irrelevant but come to mind for some reason. Don't try to decode the meaning; just put down everything you can think of. As you reach the end of the list, look for a common thread, some recurring theme. Can you see how one event, without any intention or planning on your part, influenced another? How that late-night trip to the diner led to meeting the love of your life? How a series of useless internships influenced your career choice? You will begin to see a theme, a surprisingly obvious thread that ties it all together.

Will it be clear at first? Of course not. This is just the start. But there's less intrigue to this process than we think. Your life, though a mystery, is trying to tell you something. Are you listening?

Nothing Is Wasted

At the point Mike Noland became sick, Jody considered quitting her newly launched ministry of helping people write letters to their loved ones. It was a lot of work and often discouraging. After his death, she did give up—for a while. Grief-stricken and disappointed, she let go of the dream that had once captivated her imagination and filled her with hope.

When she saw how one little workbook made a difference in the life of a dying woman, though, Jody's dream was rekindled.

In spite of the tragedies she had experienced, she would have to endure. The cost of not doing so was too great. She had seen it in the eyes of her stepdaughter, who would never know the comfort others might. The possibility of helping others avoid that pain was what kept Jody going.

"God wastes nothing," she told me during one of our phone conversations, recalling her sixteen-year career at IBM before she quit to help her husband grow his business and raise a family. All of it played a part in where she is today.

During those years at IBM, Jody was in charge of giving performance reviews to employees. She would praise and affirm things she saw in people, even when delivering difficult feedback.

"I would always try to look below the surface," she recalled. She wanted to go beyond the typical "What have you done for me lately?" conversation. "To me, it was an obvious thing that you would do for people . . . but then I realized how rare it was."

Through her workshops and speaking engagements, Jody helps people see things in the people they love that they would otherwise struggle to express. She is, in effect, using the gift of affirmation she learned at IBM.

After my seven years of working at a nonprofit, I can relate. Nothing is wasted. No job, no task, no obstacle is useless, if we are willing to see how it can fit into our calling. At times, I felt frustrated at having to do a certain task or answer yet another e-mail. It felt like I was being held back. But now I realize the truth. There isn't a day that goes by when I don't use some skill learned during those seven years. It was all preparation for what was to come. As you explore your own calling, you will be surprised by how your previous experiences are conspiring to lead you in the direction of your life's work. You just have to listen.

Listening to your life begins with doing what none of us wants to do, with what Larry Elliott chose to do and what Mike Noland didn't do. You have to imagine your own death. When your time comes, what will you regret not doing? What will you wish you had more time to do, and what will have seemed trivial? Think of what you fear losing—those are the things that matter most.

One way to deepen this awareness is to watch other people. Pay attention to those who love their lives and see what they do. What do they have that you don't? We can learn a lot from what initially looks like envy—namely, what you are missing. You might have to see someone else love their life before you can love your own. Love, after all, is what holds this all together, what sustains a calling when nothing else will. This is not petty jealousy, not if we take it one step further and do something with those feelings.

In a way, we must become children again, watching and listening to others, mimicking the behavior we admire so that we can grow. Observing everyday examples of those who did not compromise their calling but persevered through difficulties will inspire you to press on.

When in Doubt, Commit

I hope it's clear by now that this is not a passive process. You must commit to the path. And that won't always be easy.

In our world today, we have a commitment problem. Everywhere you look, it seems you can find a lack of commitment or follow-through. Leaders shirk responsibilities. Politicians blame the "other party." And many drift from one job to the next, never fully committing to any of them. On some level, we all struggle to commit to the work necessary to find our purpose. We are used to trying something out for six months to maybe a few years, then moving on. But a vocation is not like that. It's not something you try; it's someone you become.

When we do this, when we don't give ourselves fully to the work we were born to do, we do the world—and ourselves—a disservice. Commitment is necessary. It teaches us to exchange instant gratification for long-term reward and shows us that some change takes time. In learning this discipline of staying the course, our character grows. This is the payoff of patience, the joy of watching something grow that wouldn't have been had you not spent all those years sticking with it.

But it's not just about commitment; it's also about perseverance. You can't find your passion if you don't push through pain. That's what I learned from Jody Noland and what Viktor Frankl's research revealed: discovery comes with dedication. We must seek to understand our suffering with a redemptive worldview, choosing to see the greater good in spite of the evil in this world. Otherwise, the challenges we encounter will threaten to consume us, leaving us to lives of cynicism and regret. We can't get caught up in the magic of what might have been—we must move forward, pressing on when the hard times come.

There will, of course, be failure, but with that come lessons to be learned. At times, you may commit to the wrong thing, which is fine, because it's better than the alternative—nothing. Committing to the wrong thing is better than standing still.

Another strategy, and a popular one, is to not commit to anything. To hold out for better options, wait until the last minute, move restlessly from one thing to the next, and never commit to anything that could trap you. It feels like freedom but is, in fact, just another cage. When you are surrounded with unlimited opportunities, inaction seems like the safe choice. Paralyzed by fear, many choose just that—to not move, to settle. Whether it's a job as a barista or a promising position on the corporate ladder, we take it. Because the alternative—a costly journey of discovery—is too scary to consider.

Here's the truth. The risk of not committing is greater than the cost of making the wrong choice. Because when you fail, you learn. But what happens when you don't commit, when you choose to not act? Well, nothing. When you pause without intent, when you stall due to fear, you don't learn a thing. Each wrong choice grows your character and strengthens your resilience, readying you for what comes next. Failure is a friend dressed up like an enemy.

Let's be honest, though. Despite the promises of self-help literature, failing is tough. It can hurt. Picking yourself up off the ground, one rejection after another, gets difficult after a while. But if we learn to endure, choosing to see the hidden balm in the wounds of failure, we can grow from our mistakes. We can overcome our obstacles and turn tragedy into triumph. We may even be able to celebrate those setbacks and trials, the things that once seemed so daunting, knowing they are all signs that we are on our way.

The Nail in Walt Disney's Boot

Walt Disney did his best to not ask his parents for much. Elias and Flora Disney raised a frugal family in the Midwest, first as failed farmers and later as struggling business owners. But when he spotted a pair of leather boots with metal toes, young Walt had to have them. They were a practical gift, he reasoned, and would help with his job of delivering newspapers—especially when it snowed.

In a rare instance of indulgence, his parents caved. That year at Christmas, lying beneath the tree, was a pair of leather boots waiting for Walt. He wore them every day and could often be seen tramping around downtown Kansas City in them, as any proud kid with a new prized possession would do. He also kept his promise, wearing them morning and night to deliver the paper.

One spring day, just after finishing his route, Walt crossed the street to join some friends at the local soda fountain. As he did, he noticed a piece of ice lying in the middle of the street and couldn't resist the temptation to kick it. As Walt's foot collided with the block of ice, something sharp struck his boot, and a surge of pain raced up the boy's leg. Looking down to see a horseshoe nail sticking out of his boot, he screamed. The nail had penetrated the leather exterior and drove straight into his big toe, freezing his foot fast to the block of ice.

For twenty minutes, Walt cried for help—he screamed—but no one came. Finally, a wagon driver stopped and came to his aid, chipping away at the ice and taking him to the doctor. After removing the nail with a pair of pliers and administering a tetanus shot, the doctor sent Walt home without any painkillers. He would be bedridden for two weeks.

During the days that ensued, young Walt Disney had a lot to consider, including what he might do with the rest of his life. At sixteen years old, a boy growing up in the early twentieth century didn't have much time left to become a man. College was out of the question, given the Disneys' lack of means. He would not be a lawyer or a doctor. Even if his parents did have money, Walt's poor grades and inability to concentrate in school would have done him in. His prospects were limited. Would he follow in his father's footsteps or forge his own path as his elder brother Roy had done?

The break from his regular routine allowed Walt to imagine the possibilities. During those two weeks, he must have thought about many things. Perhaps he thought about his friendship with schoolmate Walter Pfeiffer, whose family had introduced him to the magic of the theater. Maybe he thought about how he loved drawing and amusing classmates with cartoons. He may have thought of the time he and his sister, Ruth, were left home alone to discover a barrel of tar outside. Walt said it would make for excellent paint, but his sister protested. After he assured her it would come off, the two proceeded to decorate the side of the house with pictures of houses and black zigzags. It never came off.

We don't know what Walt was thinking during those two weeks in bed. But what we do know, according to biographer Bob Thomas, is that by the time his foot healed and he returned to delivering papers, "he had decided to become a cartoonist."[10] What was once a diversion was now a destiny. He needed something to disrupt his comfort, something painful to make him realize what was important. It wasn't that the nail was good; it was just the means that forced him to listen. And as painful as it was, it worked.

At times we all need moments that force us to wake up, that

command our attention. These moments happen when we least expect, whether we want them to or not. Our job isn't to wait for them or wonder why they occurred but rather to see the opportunity they provide. Walt Disney used an injury to think about what he wanted to do when he grew up. In her grief, Jody Noland recognized a chance, maybe even a responsibility, to give others comfort. When Eric Miller stopped wondering why his five-year-old son got brain cancer and decided to make the most of every moment, his life and the lives of those around him were changed.

As you avail yourself to how your life may be speaking, you too must decide. Will you wallow in regret, wondering why such a thing has befallen you, or will you choose to act, making the most of your obstacle, and allow it to evolve into an opportunity? Listening is where finding your calling starts, but it's not where it ends. Our ears can only take us so far before our hands have to do the rest of the work.

TWO

Accidental Apprenticeships

The Teacher Appears When the Student Least Expects

Every single thing that has ever
happened in your life is preparing you
for a moment that is yet to come.

—Unknown

*You cannot find your calling on your own. It's
a process that involves a team of mentors.
And everywhere you look, help is available.*

Getting pregnant at twenty-three years old was just about the worst thing that could have happened to Ginny Phang. A native Singaporean who had spent her childhood between Indonesia and Singapore, she knew having a baby out of wedlock meant trouble. This unexpected turn of events would be the first in a series to change not only Ginny's life but also the lives of many other women. First, though, she had to decide what to do about this baby.

"It started with me not doing well on my exams," she told me on a Skype call late one afternoon (early morning for her). "In a place like Singapore . . . it's very academic, which means if you fail your exams or you don't do well, that's the end of your life."[1]

Feeling lost, Ginny fled to Jakarta to live with her grandparents. Having gone through a series of bad relationships, she finally met a guy who was different from the rest. He was older, more mature, and successful. He also came from a wealthy family, which was promising for a young woman who didn't have a hopeful future. Then she got pregnant.

Her immediate reaction was, "Oh my God . . . I'm going to be a mother!" Ginny had always loved children and was excited to bring a baby into the world. Her boyfriend, though, had a different reaction.

"We're going to go for an abortion," he said.

That wasn't the answer she had expected. Having accompanied two friends to their own abortions, she had always told herself she'd never do that. After a month of fighting over whether to keep the baby or not, the couple came to a point where they knew a decision had to be made. He gave Ginny an ultimatum: have an abortion, or find a new boyfriend. To sweeten the deal, if she *did* have the abortion, he would help her start a business, something she'd always wanted to do. This was Ginny's chance to make something of herself, and there might not be many others.

Abortions are illegal in Indonesia, so Ginny moved back to Singapore to figure out what to do next. After arriving home, she made an appointment to see the doctor and then postponed it a week. Still having doubts, she scheduled an abortion but spent the entire day before the procedure deliberating over whether to go through with the decision.

She prayed, cried, even went to confession. Ginny felt stuck.

"I just couldn't bring myself to do [it]," she told me. "At the same time, I didn't know how I was going to make it work." To make matters worse, her mother had also given an ultimatum. If Ginny kept the baby, she'd have to move out of her parents' house.

"In Singapore, you don't leave the house until you get married," she explained, "because of the government policies and how expensive it is."

The idea of being out on her own scared her. Not only that, but she would have to live with the guilt of having brought public shame to her family. With no job or backup plan, how would she survive?

The night before the abortion, just a few minutes before eight o'clock when Ginny was supposed to take the pill that would begin the abortion, her aunt called.

"Flush the pills," she said. "We will help you. We don't know how, but we will help you."

Those were the words Ginny was waiting to hear. She always wanted to keep the baby but just didn't know how to make it work—until that phone call. Sometimes all it takes to make a difficult decision is an affirming voice telling you what you know to be true but still need to hear. That's what a phone call at eight o'clock at night did for a young, soon-to-be mother from Singapore. Ginny flushed the pills.

"Everything just fell into place . . ." she recalled. "Someone said something that felt right."

This is a phrase Ginny uses a lot: *it just felt right*. For her, feelings are important; they're signposts to be trusted in the journey to your purpose. But even an emotion wasn't enough to sway her toward bringing a baby into the world, risking personal bankruptcy and financial failure. She had to have confirmation. At the time, plenty of people were giving her reasons why she shouldn't keep the baby, but none that made sense. When her aunt called minutes before the abortion, those were words that rang true. Confirmation came in the form of one of the few relatives who hadn't abandoned her.

In spite of the odds against her, Ginny went through with the pregnancy. For her, it was the only thing that felt right, even if it meant being rejected by family, ending a relationship, and facing public ridicule. She left home (her mother wasn't bluffing), moved in with her grandfather, whose house belonged to the same woman who had convinced her to keep her baby, and prepared to become a mother.

If you were to speak with Ginny, you would be struck immediately by her presence. She lacks any shame that should follow someone who has been through so much rejection. You can tell just from the way she carries herself that she is someone who deserves respect, and you want to give it to her. In her eyes there is a resolve that a simple "no" or a "you can't do this" is not going to stop. It was that look, which I first saw in a TEDx video, that made me respond to her e-mail. "I have a star personality," she told me. And I had to agree with her. She's a strong woman, hardened by pain and difficulty, but nonetheless full of life.

When we see someone who has succeeded in spite of tremendous odds, we are tempted to proclaim this person a "self-made" man or woman. When we do this, though, we ignore an important fact, one that is essential to anyone's success—they didn't do it alone. As I dug deeper into the complexity of Ginny's story, I realized that was the case for her too. Yes, she's a strong woman; that's impossible to miss. You can't go through what she's endured without being tough; no one could argue with that. But even strength has its shortcomings. What you might miss when you first meet Ginny Phang—and this is in no way meant to discredit her courage—is that without the support of a few important people, she wouldn't have made it.

The Accidental Apprenticeship

In the Middle Ages, a young person worked for free in exchange for experience, room, and board. The student, called an "apprentice," would live sometimes in the same house as the master, sharing meals with the craftsman's family. This was the way a person became a professional, and the process began as early as age twelve.

After completing the first stage of apprenticeship, the student, who was now called a "journeyman," could venture out and travel to other cities, working on his own. What a journeyman could not do, however, was take on apprentices. That right was reserved only for masters. In many ways, a journeyman was still a student, though now able to be paid for his work. To be a journeyman meant applying the techniques your teacher passed down to see if they worked in the real world. It was a test, to see if you had what it took to become a master. There was a certain amount of restlessness to being a journeyman. It meant you hadn't found your place in the world yet.

After a season of wandering, a journeyman had to submit a masterpiece to the local guild. If they found it worthy, the journeyman could graduate to the title of master, being accepted into the guild and finally able to take on apprentices. Then the process would start all over again.

How much time do you think this process of apprenticeship took? Based on the modern equivalents, we might guess a few months, possibly even a year or two. Not even close. Under this system, an apprentice typically worked for a minimum of seven years before venturing out on his own. Then he would spend another few years as a journeyman before finally becoming a master—if he was worthy. The entire process took about ten years. If you started training at twelve, that meant you wouldn't become a professional until your twenties. And if you started later, you might not be able to practice a trade until your thirties. That's only *if* you were lucky enough to get an apprenticeship in the first place.

Ten years. That's how long it took to master a craft. This may be difficult to grasp today, when nearly every college student has the opportunity to go through multiple internships without much practical application, but as we have seen so far, finding your calling takes time. Practice is essential not only to achieve excellence but to clarify the call itself. An apprenticeship was an excellent way of learning a skill under the guidance of someone wiser and more experienced. But these days, there is little left of the apprenticeship system, which has left an unfortunate gap in our education. With the dawn of the Renaissance, the guilds eventually declined, and the popularity of universities grew, replacing the apprenticeship with a more general education. The ancient art of diving deep into a specific craft all but disappeared.

In modern times, the responsibility for reaching your potential is often left up to the individual. This is more than a challenge; it's a cruel taunt. How can a person be all she's supposed to be if she doesn't know *who* she is, if she doesn't have some example to aspire to? Pulling ourselves up by our bootstraps can only take us so far, and despite what we've heard, there is no such thing as a self-made man. We are all products of our environment, influenced by the people we encounter and the places we live. Born into this world with zero ability, we cannot talk, much less feed or clean ourselves, on our own. We need help. Our parents begin this process of helping us grow into our God-given identities, but at some point someone else must take over.

In epic stories of old, a young hero is called away, leaving his family to begin a great adventure. But before he steps into battle to face the dragon or start a revolution, what must happen? He needs a sage, a master magician, or perhaps a retired coach. However he or she appears, the mentor's job is simple: Teach the young person how to sharpen and refine his skills. Take over where his parents left off.

But how does such a system work today? Not the way you might think.

More often than not in the life of an extraordinary person, at a certain point they encountered a guide, some coach or mentor who helped them along, investing in their abilities to help them grow into who they were born to be. Sometimes it's a single person; other times it's a group of people. Regardless, the result is an often informal process of apprenticeship, full of failure and self-doubt, but ultimately instructive.

The truth, in spite of what we might believe about remarkable people, is that you cannot master a skill on your own. Finding your calling will not happen without the aid and assistance of others. Every story of success is, in fact, a story of community. Some people will help you willingly, while others may contribute to your education on accident. But if you are wise, you can use it all. When you set out on the road to self-discovery, it will not just be you walking on that road. "No man is an island," John Donne wrote, and this is better news than we realize.[2] We are all sharing the same path as we march toward our destinies. Your journey, though unique, is full of fellow sojourners, as well as teachers who will help along the way. Your job is not to find them but to recognize them when they appear.

In many ways, apprenticeship is an extension of the parenting process. For some, a mother or father figure initiates the transition from immaturity to maturity, but eventually someone else must complete the process. At some point while we head toward our life's work, someone new and unfamiliar will have to come into our lives and speak with authority. These people often come unexpectedly and can serve a vital role in our education. So let's look at how you don't miss these accidental apprenticeships.

Like Slipping into an Old Pair of Shoes

Despite having made the decision to keep the baby, Ginny was about to enter one of the most difficult times in her life. What she needed most—the loving support of a community—would be all but absent. "I was very lonely during pregnancy, almost suicidal," she told me. "It was the only time in my life where I couldn't see beyond twenty-four hours."

Each day, Ginny would wake up, grateful for making it to another sunrise. And each night, she would cry herself to sleep, overwhelmed with anxiety. Nearly every person in her life had abandoned her. She had brought shame to her family, lost her boyfriend, and compromised her social status in a country where unwed mothers are treated as second-class citizens. Even her friends didn't know what to do with her. While they were out partying, she was preparing to be a mother. They couldn't empathize with her situation and started excluding her. Still, she knew something was right about the path she was on.

During the delivery, the nurse kept asking when Ginny wanted the epidural. At first she declined but eventually took it because she started feeling sick. At the suggestion of her aunt, Ginny wanted to have a natural birth, but no one had ever told her how to do that. So she bore her son the best that she knew how, while her mother sat in the corner as she labored. It was hard, much harder than she imagined, but she got through it and in the end had a beautiful baby boy. "The birthing process made me realize how important it is to be supported," she said, "to have someone believe in you and protect you—how important it is to keep women safe."

That was just the beginning. Though she didn't know it at the time, the whole experience, even the pain of childbirth, would soon play an important role in Ginny's life.

After the birth, she went back to her job as an office secretary, which provided some stability but wasn't enough to satisfy her. The position provided steady hours and flexibility to spend time with her son, but the pay wasn't great and she was sure this wasn't what she was supposed to be doing with her life. "I was bored," she said. "I couldn't see myself living this way for the rest of my life." But she wasn't about to give up. In spite of the taboos that surrounded her situation, she wanted respect and wasn't afraid to break convention to get it.

Partly out of curiosity and partly due to boredom, Ginny started an online business educating mothers on the health benefits of breastfeeding. She and her peers had grown up on formula, and as a result, very few Singaporean mothers knew much about nursing. Through her online store, she sold T-shirts and other products advocating breastfeeding awareness. She had seen the positive effects of nursing her own child and wanted to help other mothers who were interested in more natural approaches to child rearing. Although she wasn't much of an online shopper herself, the experience opened up a whole new world to her.

Since she was usually working or taking care of her son, most of Ginny's socialization happened through a network of friends she had met on the Internet. One friend, Amy, was an Australian Chinese woman who had been successful working as a doula in Singapore. Since she was the only Asian doing that sort of work, the locals trusted her. One night when they were talking, Amy said something to Ginny that would change her life.

"Ginny, you will make a good doula."

"What's a doula?" I asked Ginny. "A birth coach," she told me, someone who helps a mother create a plan for how she is going to handle the birth of her child. When she heard this, it took Ginny by surprise, because back then she didn't know what a doula was either. She didn't have one at her own child's birth and had no idea what doulas did. Her friend added that whether she became a doula or not, taking the class would be a good experience.

"I've always been a fan of personal development," Ginny told me.

So she signed up and took the class, learning all the things that doulas did. But when it came time to attend her first birth, Ginny forgot what to do. She panicked. Taking a deep breath, Ginny let "her spirit take over" and tried to focus, remembering her training.

She started by massaging the mother's back, then comforted her through the experience, assuring her that everything was going to be all right. It worked. This wasn't the mother's first child, but it was her first delivery without drugs, and she was scared. Afterward the mother was elated, crediting Ginny for how relaxed she felt and how easy the experience was.

"It was exhilarating," Ginny recalled, "like slipping into an old pair of shoes."

That's when she knew she could do this. Shortly after that first delivery, her friend Amy left Singapore, almost as mysteriously as she had entered Ginny's life in the first place. It wasn't the most traditional model for mentoring, but it was the apprenticeship Ginny needed. And as we will see, that's usually how the process works.

Multiple Mentors

Mentoring is an easy word to throw around these days. You'll hear it tossed into conversation amongst friends or casually mentioned between business colleagues over coffee. But mentoring is much easier to talk about than it is to practice.

Why is it so difficult to find a mentor? To begin with, you're dealing with people: flawed human beings who each have their own expectations and agendas. We all have our own issues, and one of the reasons it can be so hard to find a good mentor these days is that so few people have been mentored. We have believed the myth of the self-made man and have given in to the illusion of self-reliance. What we need is something to pull us out of our own independence and arrogance. Which means the mentor that comes might not be the one we were expecting.

Chances are, your apprenticeship will not look like you imagined. Your mentor may not be the teacher you dreamed of, and that's the point. This is your education of what is, not what you think should be. A teacher who challenges you, who doesn't meet your expectations, who forces you to think and act differently, is exactly what you need. That is, after all, the job of an educator.

"The teacher appears when the student is ready" is a nice-sounding cliché, but the truth is the student is *never* ready. Throughout our lives, we will encounter a number of people who will appear at times, ready to instruct, and it will be our job to recognize them.

In my life, I've had many mentors: from my college chaplain, to my first boss, to the guy who lives down the street from us and sometimes helps me fix things. Most of the time, I've failed to recognize the importance of these relationships until well after they were over. Sometimes, their influence was subtle and undetected. Other times, it was clear they were trying to invest in me; I was just too stubborn to appreciate it. In every example, though, I would have benefited more from the mentor had I been intentional about the process.

Throughout this process of finding your life's work, you must be willing to look for mentors in unexpected places. Your friends, long-lost relatives, even old relationships that have dwindled down may become the sources of inspiration you need. Each person serves a purpose: some will arrive at just the right time to cheer you on, while others are there to identify with the struggles you're living. And even others will show up when you need them the most. All of these people in their own way are mentors, contributing to your apprenticeship.

How do you find these people? Where do they come from? It's hard to tell. Likely they'll surprise you, appearing seemingly out of nowhere at just the right time. The whole thing will look like an accident or a mystery but, of course, it is far from it. As Paulo Coelho writes, "When you want something, all the universe conspires in helping you to achieve it."[3] There's some truth to that. Fortune favors the motivated. When a person is determined to not just succeed but to do work that matters, the world makes room for such ambition. You won't be able to predict how this apprenticeship unfolds, but you can be prepared for it when it comes.

Ginny Phang could have easily missed her calling had she not heeded her friend Amy's advice to take the doula class. She may not have been ready for what would be required of her, but she was ready to take action. And that small step made all the difference.

I often hear people who need guidance in their lives asking for advice on how to find a mentor, but that's the wrong question to ask. When you pursue a calling, you will find a community of supporters to champion you along the way. It's not up to you where these people come from or even how to locate them. You just need to keep your eyes open. Accidental apprenticeships are all around you, and if you listen to your life you'll be able to recognize them.

The Resurgence of Apprenticeship

In East Hampton, New York, Ellen Frank is reviving a practice the world hasn't seen since the Renaissance. In her small studio, she is teaching a handful of interns the art of illumination, a technique that involves using gold to embellish sacred documents. The studio is called the Illumination Atelier and is a haven for live-in artists who want to work under the guidance of a true master.

Atelier is a French word meaning "workshop," and during the Middle Ages these were the main areas of education for artists. In such a workshop, the master artist, often accompanied by assistants and apprentices, would create works that would go out in the master's name. It was a collaborative effort, which allowed the artist to produce more work and provide a learning experience for the fledgling artists.

Ateliers often worked in collaboration with local guilds, which controlled the apprenticeship process, and although they still exist in a few places around the world today, their popularity has dramatically declined. To Ellen Frank, this is a tragedy. Her small workshop is an opportunity to share her passion for not only art but also peace and reconciliation.

After a trip to Jerusalem in 1999, where she experienced a land in turmoil, Ellen was inspired to create a large-scale piece using the illumination project.[4] While designing the invitation to a celebration party for the exhibit, she had "a moment of grace,"[5] realizing she wanted to continue exploring these themes of peace and cultural understanding in her work. She started a foundation, which provides support and housing for interns who want to learn illumination. Since 2005, she has been finding interns on Craigslist from more than fifteen different countries and inviting them to work in her studio.

In Ellen's studio, interns are involved in the whole process: from imagining the initial concept of a piece, to the creation of it, to even important business decisions that have to be made for the foundation. They always get their names added to the work they do.

The decline of the atelier, according to Ellen, has meant a decline in artistic technique and craft. Her little atelier is trying to fix that. "I think we bring back an intimacy of mentorship and training where the apprentice . . . learns directly from the experienced artist," she said in an interview with National Public Radio. "They also acquire validation. It's not teaching through critique. It's not teaching through judging their own work. It's teaching through saying, 'Yes, and why not try this?' and, 'Yes, can you push this further?'"[6]

When Ellen teaches, her voice is gentle, almost motherly, as she guides her students through the technique. With soothing words of affirmation and phrases that build anticipation, like "this is the magic moment," she helps you feel the significance of what you're doing, which in turn leads to confidence.[7] Some interns, she admits, have even become better than she is at certain techniques. This is the power of the process. A good apprenticeship isn't about an exchange of information; it's about passing on the skill of the master and multiplying it.

This small studio is just the beginning. Ellen's real dream is an "open atelier" where all kinds of people, not just artists, can come and learn.[8] As I listened to the radio tell her story, it was hard to not think education should look more like this—paint splotches and messy smocks in a cramped studio—and less like large lecture halls with passive students parked in seats for ninety minutes at a time, eyes glued to a slide presentation.

Can you imagine a world where school looked more like an atelier and less like an auditorium? In some areas, that's not quite so unrealistic.

Germany has one of the lowest unemployment rates in Western Europe. The reason for this is its "dual system," which involves young adults enrolling in vocational schools that allow them to split their time between study and work. In this system, a student might work a few days per week with the business and then spend the rest of his time at school. Unlike most internships, these students get paid a percentage of a full-time worker's wages, and 90 percent of them complete their programs. About half of those people continue working with the company after the apprenticeship is over.

The experience is a taste of employment that not only adds value to the company but also gives the student an education he can then use in the real world. Unlike other parts of the world where unemployment is skyrocketing, Germany has a shortage of workers. A good job is available for anyone who is qualified and willing to work. What's lacking are the workers. Maybe this is true in other parts of the world, as well. We don't need more jobs. We need a better way to equip people for what they're meant to do. In the case of Germany, such a system seems to be creating more jobs than it can handle.[9]

An apprenticeship is designed to give you guidance from an expert, knowledge in a given field, and experience in a challenging environment, all of which prepare you for your future. But such an experience, as promising as it sounds, is not easy. It takes a lot of courage and tenacity to not only find but also finish an apprenticeship.

Life is complicated and messy, not often looking like the textbook told us. Most of us struggle to find our way, and we are desperate for guidance, which often seems unavailable. It can be tempting to check out and choose a seemingly safer path. The chance to do work that matters is a choice. Opportunities to learn and grow are available, if we're willing to look in the right places and humbly accept what we find.

Use Your Environment: The Steve Jobs Strategy

Every place you go, every person you meet, every job you have is a chance to gain greater clarity in your self-education. Life is the classroom, and if you are paying attention, you can recognize the daily lessons available. Each day is a new page in a textbook you never complete, and as you sit in the student's seat, you realize the apprenticeship has already begun.

The smart way to begin this process is by practicing with the tools available to you. Traditional mentors are hard to come by, but you already have access to wisdom and experience, teachers who will guide you in making decisions that will help you find your way. Who can you call on the phone and talk to right now? What friend or former coach would meet you for coffee this week if you asked? We all want to find someone who wants to invest in us, someone who cares, without realizing those people are already in our lives. The worst way to get a mentor is to go find one. The best way is to see the one that's already there.

Ginny Phang spent years trying to find her way, barely surviving. She wasn't searching for some great calling; she was fighting for her life. But this is how we encounter our life's work: in the midst of some other pursuit, while striving to pay the bills or simply make it through another day. At some point, though, something unexpected appears and changes everything. And often that something is a some*one*. The teacher appears when you least expect.

For Ginny, a few people served as guides in her journey.

First there was the aunt who encouraged her to keep her son and gave her a place to stay. Then there was Amy, the friend who told Ginny she'd be a good doula, convincing her to undergo the training. Finally there was the producer who filmed a documentary on unwed mothers in Singapore and became Ginny's roommate. As Ginny's business grew, her roommate helped her by watching the baby and taking care of administrative responsibilities, such as building her first website. Without the support of these people, Ginny admitted, "I wouldn't be where I am today."

Each person had a different role to play and helped in a unique way, appearing at just the right time when she needed it. This model looks vastly different from the Renaissance version of apprenticeship but accomplishes the same result. An accidental apprenticeship begins with listening to your life and paying attention to the ways in which you're already being prepared for your life's work. Ginny's success wasn't in that she planned any of this out; it was that when the opportunities came, she acknowledged them and took action.

This was how Steve Jobs, the cofounder of Apple Computer, got his start. His own education was almost entirely informal, beginning with a short stint at Reed College, where the classes were so expensive he decided to drop out after six months. Sleeping on the floors of friends' dorm rooms, he stayed on campus and continued to audit a few classes, including a calligraphy course, which he later credited for influencing the beautiful typography used in the first Mac.

Later, Jobs became friends with Steve Wozniak, who, before they founded Apple together, helped him get a job at Atari. "Woz" had redesigned an earlier version of the game Pong, which Jobs passed off as his own work to get hired as a technician.

While working at Atari, Jobs, who was hard to get along with, learned important lessons about design, software development, and creating technology for consumers. With every opportunity, he gained guidance, knowledge, and experience—each from a different source—all of which he was able to use later in life with Apple and Pixar.[10]

Rarely do you find all the elements of an apprenticeship in one place. But if you look in the right places and are careful to pay attention, you *will* find them. Apprenticeship, then, isn't a class you take or a mentor you meet—it's a choice you make. And in that case, an accidental apprenticeship isn't much of an accident at all; it's the intentional process of choosing the opportunities you need to create your life's work.

Unlike a formal education, this option is available to anyone. Instead of waiting for a teacher to come choose you or an academic institution to accept you, this apprenticeship is ready to begin when you are.

From Apprentice to Master

When Ginny Phang's boss saw her on a full-page feature in the national newspapers, he didn't like it. Unwed pregnancy is a taboo subject in Singapore, and most unmarried mothers don't talk about their situation, much less appear on TV. Those willing to talk, therefore, tend to get a lot of attention.

Believing in the power of education to dispel ignorance, Ginny started making appearances on any documentary, current affairs program, or news show that would have her. She would tell her story and share what she was doing. It didn't take long for her boss to find out what she was up to. Upset, he told her she would have to choose between her newfound passion and her stable job. He even offered her more money to stick with the day job.

"I came to a crossroads where I had to decide," Ginny said. "Am I going to do this job that gives me certainty, or take the leap of faith and venture into a place that's never been explored in Singapore?"[11]

At the time, there were no full-time doulas in Singapore. Ginny's Australian friend Amy had left the country, and the few remaining doulas were only working part-time. Nobody knew whether or not a person could make a living off this kind of work. It was quite a gamble. "Leap, and the net will appear" is a saying we sometimes hear in reference to such situations.[12] The idea behind the phrase is that when you are backed into a corner, an impossible solution will present itself. At the times when you feel stuck, the right thing to do is take a risk and go "all in" with whatever the scariest option might be. So that's just what Ginny did. She took the leap.

Fast-forward ten years. Ginny now runs Four Trimesters, a full-time doula business and the largest company of its kind in Singapore, with seven employees. She has been featured on TV programs and in news articles and has had the opportunity to speak at a TEDx event. Hers is a story of defying the odds, of persevering until passion became reality. If there ever were such a thing as a self-made woman, Ginny is it. But did she really do it all on her own?

She would be the first to tell you no. It was difficult to get that ultimatum from her boyfriend and even harder having her mother throw her out of the house. Those were difficult experiences and are still painful memories. Even now, a decade later, she gets cross looks from strangers when they learn she's not married.

If you were to ask Ginny when she was a little girl what she wanted to be, she wouldn't have said "a doula." That idea hadn't even occurred to her until someone else suggested it. She always wanted to run her own business but didn't know how to make that happen. Through a series of accidents, though, she found her way. It wasn't by design (not her design, anyway) and she didn't understand what was happening as the events were unfolding, but with the help of a handful of people, Ginny was guided to her calling.

"At five years old, I wanted to be a dancer and a business woman," Ginny wrote me in an e-mail. "By thirteen, I thought I would make a good counselor and was told that I would be a good radio DJ. Now in my thirties, I am still unfolding and can see all my childhood dreams materializing in my work as a doula."[13]

There's something to be said for the power of perseverance and a person's will to survive. Certainly Ginny's story is a testament to the ability of the human spirit to endure. But it's also a testament to the power of community, a reminder that we never find a calling on our own. We all need help.

Years ago, when deciding whether or not to keep her baby, Ginny never could have imagined where she would be now, helping other women have the support she never received as a new mother. What makes her story special, though, is not that she got help—help is always available when we need it. It's that she recognized it when it came.

Remember: this all began because Ginny didn't do well on her exams. It wasn't an exceptional education that brought her to this place. It was a series of unexpected incidents and unlikely mentors that created the perfect opportunity to grow. An accidental apprenticeship is like that. These experiences are impossible to engineer but easy to recognize once you know what to look for.

Sometimes the people who help us find our calling come from the least likely of places. It's our job to notice them.

THREE

Painful Practice

When Trying Isn't Good Enough

Always do more than is required of you.

—George S. Patton

Your calling is not always easy. It will take work. Practice can teach you what you are and are not meant to do.

Stephanie Fisher had come a long way from her hometown of Jamestown, New York, to Augusta, Georgia—777 miles, to be exact—but this was her dream and she wouldn't give it up. The year was 2010, and it was her seventh time auditioning for *American Idol.* She had never made it this far in the singing talent show, but this time, things were going to be different. This time, she would see the judges.

The twenty-three-year-old college graduate with degrees in biochemistry and communication studies was determined to make this audition a success and get invited to Hollywood Week, where dozens of contestants would compete for a chance at the finals. In the middle of pursuing a master's degree while working part-time as a model, she figured there was little time left to chase her dream of becoming a singer. It was now or never.

"I only have four more years of entertainment in my life," she told a local newspaper just before the audition, "and if I have the opportunity to do it, I might as well take that."[1]

Dressed in a silvery sequined top, donning pearls around her neck and fishnet stockings, Stephanie stepped onto the platform of America's most popular talent show, smiling nervously before the judges.

"Wow," a couple of them said, remarking on her outfit.

"I almost wore the same thing," Randy joked.

Simon rolled his eyes, obviously annoyed.

"Okay," Kara said, "let's hear it."

In her black and white oxfords, Stephanie spread her feet apart as if to ready herself, and she opened with Peggy Lee's "Fever."

"Never know how much I love you / Never know how much I care . . ."

At this point, Stephanie was snapping her fingers and provocatively staring down the judges, who were audibly groaning. Her rhythm was off, the notes were wrong, and everyone on the set knew it, including Stephanie.

They told her to stop. She frowned.

"Thank you, Stephanie," Simon said.

"What did you think?" Kara asked.

"Terrible. Honestly, you can't sing, sweetheart."

In the YouTube video that tells her painful story over and over again, Stephanie admitted to being a little starstruck in the presence of Victoria Beckham, who was a guest judge that day. Later she told a reporter this was something the producers told her to say. Victoria offered to turn around in hopes that it would make the contestant feel more at ease. Stephanie accepted the offer, which felt forced and a little too theatrical for me.

The young grad student started again, a little more awkwardly, this time singing "Baby Love" by The Supremes. It wasn't any better. After a measure or two, Victoria turned back around. This time Kara added to the critical jabs, saying it was better when she *was* looking. Another burst of laughter erupted from the judges.

"With the greatest respect," Simon said in a proper British accent, pausing for dramatic effect, "you have a horrible voice."

"Really?" Stephanie said, looking stunned but still smiling nervously. All the preparation, all those long years of dreaming, had led to *this*?

"Yeah," Randy chimed sympathetically. "You ain't got it goin' on."

"You can't give me a few minutes to get un-nervous?" she pleaded.

"We'd need *years*, Stephanie," Simon said, and the judges again all laughed in unison.[2]

And as I watched from the anonymity of my home office years after the fact, I realized how much truth there was in that statement.

The Myth of Talent

It's a typical story. If you're familiar with any talent show, you know it well. Young dreamer waiting her whole life for a shot at the big time leaves home in search of an opportunity. When she gets the chance, she steps into the spotlight and proceeds to completely bomb, all in front of a live audience. It's painful but entertaining to watch, and we all feel a slight twinge of guilt for amusing ourselves at someone else's expense.

The most painful part, though, is the fight that often ensues after the rejection. The judges tell the talent she doesn't have what it takes, and she protests: "I don't understand . . . I've been practicing my whole life . . . I hired a vocal coach . . . This is my dream . . . Everyone says I can sing . . ." On one show, I saw a middle-aged man who was voted off proceed to disagree with the judges, saying he had been practicing with a choreographer for three hours a night, and they simply didn't know what they were talking about.

We know the tale well. It's the stuff prime-time entertainment is made of. But what about when the opposite happens—when an unknown person takes the stage and, much to the amazement of the critics, blows everyone away?

That's what Susan Boyle did when she appeared on *Britain's Got Talent* in 2009. A middle-aged woman with a thick Scottish accent, modest appearance, and a bit of an attitude, Susan was not what the judges expected. By the end of "I Dreamed a Dream" from *Les Miserables*, she had received a standing ovation. How is it that one person over the course of thirty seconds can astound an audience, becoming the next international pop sensation, while someone else cannot? What's the difference?

The traditional answer, and the reason such shows exist in the first place, is that the person doesn't have any talent. Forget passion and go find something you're good at. "You're really smart," Kara told Stephanie, while trying to let the young lady down gently and point her in a more productive direction.[3]

But how, then, do we explain the success of Hillary Scott, who auditioned for *American Idol* twice but failed to make it to the judges' round both times, and then went on to form the group Lady Antebellum? Lady A is one of the most popular music groups in the world, having won seven Grammys in their career. And what about pop singer Colbie Caillat, who was also rejected twice on *American Idol,* ironically singing her future hit "Bubbly," which went on to help her sell more than six million albums and ten million singles?[4] If the answer were as easy as "you don't have enough talent," then Scott and Caillat would have had reason to give up. But they didn't, and perseverance paid off—at least for them. So maybe there is more to the issue than talent.

Over the past several years, researchers have argued that what we used to think of as natural talent is, in fact, the result of good old-fashioned practice. Author of *Talent Is Overrated,* Geoff Colvin, wrote, "Talent means nothing like what we think it means, if indeed it means anything at all."[5] Citing numerous studies of accomplished individuals, world-class athletes, and performers whom we often consider prodigies, he claimed the reason for their success was practice. When the evidence does point to rare instances of natural ability, he argued, it was always followed by rigorous training. "Such findings do not prove that talent doesn't exist," he wrote. "But they do suggest an intriguing possibility: that if it does, it may be irrelevant." In other words, nobody reaches expert status without intense preparation. Excellence, then, is a matter of practice, not talent.[6]

Two-time Grammy winner Colbie Caillat testified to this, admitting the *Idol* judges were right to reject her: "I was shy. I was nervous. I didn't look the greatest. I wasn't ready for it yet. I was glad, when I auditioned, that they said no."[7] Did you catch that? She was glad, grateful even, for the rejection. It made her try harder and helped her understand she was not performing at her very best. The failure made her better.

Is there a difference between Stephanie Fisher and the *American Idol* rejects who went on to become superstars? If it's not talent, then what *is* it? Does practice alone explain the gap between reality show rejects and future pop stars? Or is there a deeper question we ought to be asking? We all know someone whose passion exceeds their skill and who, for no lack of trying, can't seem to break through. What advice do we offer such people? Can we honestly stare them in the face and say, "Try harder"? Something about that seems wrong.

Didn't Stephanie try? It sure seems that way. And it'd be hard to argue with her effort: she didn't quit after seven rejections. But maybe the problem wasn't the amount of practice she was doing. Maybe it was the *kind* of practice.

The Effort Excuse

Our parents told us to try. "It doesn't matter how well you do," my dad used to tell me while looking at my report card, "just that you did your best."

I went through much of life explaining a lack of excellence with that very excuse: *I gave it my best.* This became my default shrug-it-off response whenever facing failure. "At least I tried." What more could anyone ask?

I used the Effort Excuse whenever encountering a challenge that exceeded my abilities, like playing the saxophone, for instance. I halfheartedly attempted to play the woodwind instrument for six months before finally quitting in frustration. It was just too difficult, or maybe I just wasn't that interested. What I was doing felt like trying, like I was doing my best. But it wasn't. I was confusing my understanding of ability with what was actually possible.

For many of us, there is a fundamental problem with our understanding of our own capabilities. We are often exceeding our own expectations of ourselves. And in spite of the evidence pointing to the contrary, we continue to believe in the Myth of Talent, that some people are born a certain way, that we cannot rise above our circumstances and achieve something greater than we've ever done before. When we do this, we deceive ourselves.

I gave up playing the saxophone before pushing myself to the limits of my ability. I know this, because when I started playing guitar the same thing happened. After six months of "trying," I wanted to quit, but this time my dad wouldn't let me. Whenever I would get into trouble, he would ground me from all activities *except* playing the guitar. "If you want to listen to music," he would say, "you'll have to play it yourself." Sure, I was being disciplined for whatever wrong I had committed, but he was also putting me in a position that forced me to grow, and it worked. After only months of practicing, of pushing through that six-month dip, I was playing the riffs I had grown up listening to, better than I ever thought possible.

Surely the same has happened to you. At some point you did something you didn't believe you could do, something th surprised you. Maybe a coach encouraged you or a parent pushed you or in a moment of inspiration you motivated yourself. But you dug a little deeper, increased your dedication, and somehow accomplished the impossible—all because you changed the way you thought. Hardwired in our brains and bodies is a potential greater than we realize, and all we have to do to unlock it is believe.

Psychology professor Carol Dweck has written about this, explaining why some people respond to rejection differently than others, saying the difference between the successful and unsuccessful often comes down to mindset.[8]

According to Dweck, most people adhere to one of two mindsets: the fixed mindset or the growth mindset. With the fixed mindset, people are born with a certain number of finite abilities and cannot exceed those abilities. With the growth mindset, however, potential is unlimited. You can always get better. For this kind of person, the goal is not so much to be the best in the world but to be better than you were yesterday. Regardless of natural talent or the lack thereof, every person has the ability to improve themselves.[9]

When my dad told me to do my best, he wasn't setting me up for disappointment. He was teaching me a valuable lesson about life—it's more important to try than to rest on your natural ability. Why? Because you're capable of more than you realize, and in trying, you learn something new as you push past possibility. As a result, you grow, learning that most skills are not inborn, but ~~~ Practiced. At least, they can be, if you're willing to adopt ~~~dset and dedicate yourself to the practice that fol~~~most gifted people do not have what it takes to ~~~t the right attitude and years of practice.

More Than Mindset

Did Stephanie Fisher have the right mindset? Was she not focused enough? Did she not believe enough? Or was there some other thing she was lacking?

The term *deliberate practice* was first coined by K. Anders Ericsson, a Swedish psychologist at the University of Florida whose research claimed that talent is not the cause of excellence—practice is. But not just any kind of practice, he said—a specific kind of practice that leads to expert performance.[10]

In an era of human history in which we prize comfort above nearly every other virtue, we have overlooked an important truth: comfort never leads to excellence. What it takes to become great at your craft is practice, but not just any kind of practice—the kind that hurts, that stretches and grows you. This kind of practice, which Ericsson called "deliberate" and we might consider more appropriately as "painful," is extremely difficult. It takes place over the course of about ten years, or ten thousand hours—incidentally the average length of an apprenticeship. But this is not where the practice ends; it's just where it begins. In other words, you don't clock in ten thousand hours and instantly become an expert. You have to do the right kind of practice.

According to Daniel Coyle, author of a book called *The Talent Code*, the right kind of practice is a process of repeated tasks that end in failure. You fail and fail and fail again until you finally succeed and learn not only the right way to do something, but the *best* way.[11] This is what he calls "deep practice," and it's the reason why putting in just enough time will only get you so far. To master any skill, you must first choose a task; then do it over and over again until the activity becomes second nature; and finally, push through the times when you fail, exhibiting even greater focus as you repeat the action until you've done it right.[12]

Most of us have believed that all it takes to get good at something is time. If you put enough hours in, eventually you will be great. But this isn't always true. In Ericsson's research, ten thousand hours of practice was a common characteristic amongst world-class performers, but it was not the *only* characteristic. If anything, ten thousand hours is more a description of expert performance than a prescription for how anyone can achieve expertise. Every performer in the study embodied a certain *kind* of practice. It wasn't just the quantity of hours they accumulated but the quality of practice they did.

This kind of practice is a deep work that brings world-class athletes and musicians to the edge of their abilities and then takes them one step further.[13] Understanding the distinction between ordinary and extraordinary practice will help us understand why Stephanie Fisher continued to fail, why Colbie Caillat eventually didn't, and why pursuing your calling is supposed to be difficult.

It's easy to practice when the activity is something we enjoy, but what do you do when the excitement runs out and your strength disappears? What do you do when that first thrill of entering a new vocation begins to wane? Do you give up? Or do you push through the pain and make your way to mastery? This is where experts differ from the rest of us. They recognize the resistance we all feel but instead choose to see it as a sign of how close they are to their goal. Disciplining themselves, they deliberately lean in to the most difficult parts when most people tend to quit. We have come to call these people "geniuses" and "prodigies" without ever fully understanding the work that it takes to reach such a status. But the truth is, what's in them just might be in all of us.

Have you ever tried something and completely failed the first time? Remember wiping out so badly you never wanted to try again, never wanted to get back on the bike or ask another person out on a date? We understand that some skills take time and none of us knows how to do certain things without a little failure. Pain is instructive to the person willing to learn. But do we apply the same lesson to our vocations? Usually not.

As children, we are courageous and willing to fail, but as we get older, we acquire inhibitions. Our shame reflex kicks in. Unwilling to try new things, we settle for *good* when called to greatness. Why do we do this? Because it's easy. To push ourselves past what others expect, beyond what is normal, is difficult and sometimes awkward. But it is a necessary part of the process.

What does it take to develop the habits that lead to excellence? How do we not just answer our callings but master them? There are three requirements for deliberate practice, according to Ericsson and his team of researchers. First, the practice requires a context: time and energy from the individual as well as trainers, teaching materials, and facilities in which to train.[14]

Second, the activity must not be "inherently motivating." It has to be something you wouldn't naturally enjoy doing.[15] Think of it this way: if the practice is enjoyable, then you aren't growing. Muscle grows through strain and stress that create tiny tears in the muscle fiber and cause it to expand. Skills and knowledge are developed the same way. This is why so few people engage in the process of painful practice. It's hard. But, as Tom Hanks says in *A League of Their Own*, "It's supposed to be hard. If it wasn't hard, everyone would do it. The hard is what makes it great."[16]

Third, the activity cannot be done a very long time without leading to exhaustion. You must take yourself beyond what you think is possible, to the utter limits of your ability. If you aren't pushing yourself to the point of sheer exhaustion, you're not trying hard enough.[17]

Now contrast this paradigm of practice with my regular running habit, which I usually do a few times a week if I'm lucky. It's fun, easy, and keeps me in shape, but will it lead to world-class performance? Not likely. I haven't put nearly enough hours in, not to mention the right kind of hours. I only run when it's convenient, never pushing myself too hard. Why *don't* I put more effort into exercise? Because I don't want to. It's something I do for fun, not excellence.

This is an important distinction when considering your life's work. Most people won't continue doing something they aren't passionate about, especially when it gets hard. Putting an activity through painful practice is a great way to determine your direction in life. If you can do something when it's *not* fun, even when you're exhausted and bored and want to give up, then it just might be your calling.

I don't know where this idea that your calling is supposed to be easy comes from. Rarely do easy and greatness go together. The art of doing hard things requires an uncommon level of dedication. You have to love the work to be able to persevere through those difficult times, those painful moments when you would probably rather quit. How do you do that without an uncanny amount of passion? It's not possible. You must love the work. Not until you find something you can do to the point of exhaustion, to the extent that you almost hate it but can return to it tomorrow, have you found something worth pursuing.

Love, I think, is a much better criterion than lack of difficulty. If you can love what you do, even when it hurts, then you may have more than a hobby. And if you've never pushed your talents this far before, if you've never tested your skills that much, then you probably haven't discovered your true vocation. Sometimes, the only way to know the difference between a hobby and a calling is to put yourself through the crucible of painful practice.

What a Prodigy Doesn't Look Like

When I think of Martyn Chamberlin, a single word comes to mind: *prodigy*. A precocious twenty-one-year-old web developer running his own company as a senior in college, he looks like the poster child for the next Microsoft or Google. Seeing his sudden success, you might be tempted to think of him as a young Bill Gates. Like me, you might assume he must have been using a computer his whole life. And you would be wrong.

The truth is Martyn had only used the family computer for schoolwork before the age of sixteen. But in just a short amount of time, he learned Photoshop, familiarized himself with HTML and CSS, and started charging for web design services. In less than two years, he built a blog, started a business, and began attracting clients to earn money for college. What might surprise you is that long before he was a web developer, Martyn was an artist, and he never would have imagined himself spending his days staring at a computer screen.[18]

Martyn's story is not one of long-term preparation for some big moment, but rather a testimony of how powerful a spark of inspiration can be at just the right time, and how practice can happen even without our even knowing it.

A homeschool kid growing up in the home of a Baptist minister, Martyn didn't have much access to the one computer in the Chamberlin house. So he spent his free time painting and playing guitar. When his brother William left their hometown of Bixby, Oklahoma, to attend the University of Tulsa in 2008, he left the family computer open for his younger brother to use. "Before then," Martyn recalled in a phone conversation, "I rarely touched a computer because he was always on it." Just before William left, Martyn told his brother he wanted to build websites for people, so William gave him a book on the subject.

When I asked him where the desire to build websites came from, he said it probably came from watching his brother. "A case of younger brother syndrome, I guess," Martyn said. "William was smart, going to college. I was a starving artist who wasn't living in reality. I realized I needed to make a name for myself if I was ever going to attract the kinds of people I wanted to spend my life with. Plus, I loved design." Still, he was unsure of the future.

When he was eighteen, Martyn took a trip from Oklahoma to California to attend a painting workshop, where he created an eleven-by-fourteen-inch "oil on linen" painting, which was featured in the Zantman Art Gallery in Carmel. At the time, he thought this was his big break, what would finally launch his art career. But when he started posting his artwork online, he not only unlocked a passion he never knew he had; he also saw a demand for a new skill.

When Martyn started working on websites, it was first just a hobby but then developed into something more. His initial website was a replica of BubbleUnder.com, a tutorial in the book his brother gave him, which he never published. His second project was a personal home page, a site showing his art portfolio. The third was a website for an Australian client who ended up never using it but paid Martyn $800 nonetheless. It was his first paying gig. "It taught me that people were willing to pay for my skill set," he recalled.

As Martyn put his work out there for the world to see, he noticed how visitors to his website started showing more interest in his design services than his oil paintings. After building that first website, he felt exhilarated. "It made me feel like I had just made something important," he said. Not unlike the feeling he experienced after finishing a painting. "Something just clicked."

Now, a few years later, Martyn runs his own web design company, which helps pay the bills while he finishes up school. Every time he works on a website, he uses skills he acquired as an artist. Concepts like color theory, composition, and the golden triangle help him create better sites for clients—skills he learned long before he ever starting building websites. Never would he have guessed all those years of painting were actually training him for something that wasn't art, at least not in the traditional sense.

So how did a young man who dreamed of becoming an artist turn into a web developer? How did someone who didn't grow up playing computer games start a business building websites? And how did he learn all those skills so quickly? The easy answer is to say he was called. But as we have seen, a calling is never so simple. The more complex answer, the honest one, is that before he knew what he was doing, Martyn was practicing.

The lesson of the Accidental Apprenticeship is that long before a person is ready for his calling, life is preparing that person for the future through chance encounters and serendipitous experiences. That's what Martyn's brother William was doing. He was mentoring his little brother, without even knowing it, in a skill that would eventually be instrumental in his success. Neither brother probably knew the significance of what was happening, but the two were engaged in a long-distance apprenticeship in which the elder was influencing the younger, helping him find his way.

But Martyn didn't stop with watching his brother. He absorbed all the content available to him, reading everything he could find on the subject—blogs, articles, books, anything. His goal wasn't just to be good; he wanted to be great. When working on a website, especially at the beginning, if he came across a problem he couldn't solve, he would look up the answer online and figure it out. "I used to joke, saying, 'I'm not a good programmer,'" he said. "I'm just really good at using Google.' There was a lot of truth to this."

All humility aside, when Martyn got serious, he acquired a skill most people cannot fathom figuring out. And he did it in just a couple of years. He didn't study abstract information or pay thousands of dollars for classes with outdated information he'd never use. He used his previous experience, got to work, and asked for help along the way. He practiced.

The way Martyn Chamberlin found his calling, or at least the start of it, was an accident. His brother gave him a book that unlocked a skill he never knew he had and opened up a world of possibility. He watched what someone else did, got a vision for his future, and spent hours every day working toward that goal. It's not that he knew he wanted to design websites. He didn't. He just loved art and stumbled upon an application of that passion that surprised him. Trying something new, he discovered that he was good at building websites and enjoyed it.

True practice is not just about learning a skill; it's about investing the time and energy necessary to discern if this is what you are meant to do. It's about using difficulty to discover what resonates and what does not. And as you see what does, you will take one more step in the right direction.

It Starts with a Spark

Aren't we discrediting luck a little, though? Don't some people succeed just because they get a big break when others do not? Certainly we can't deny the existence of special opportunities for some people. The idea that every person can be whatever he or she wants isn't always true. Success is more than a matter of hard work; it's contingent on factors sometimes outside of our control. Where and when you were born can influence what you do.

But greatness does not just happen—Ericsson's research and

common sense tell us that. Skill is the result of intense practice; it's the product of persistent trial and error until the person gets it right. Nobody walked on to the set of *American Idol* and blew away the judges without practicing, and nobody picked up a computer and started coding. It takes a lot of practice to get good.

There are, however, times when practice is not enough, as with Stephanie Fisher's seven auditions. And there are surprising moments of breakthrough, as with Martyn Chamberlin, when a person picks up a skill on the first try as if he were born for it.

Maybe he was.

What we are learning from science now is that although humans are capable of more than anybody thought a hundred years ago, there *are* some abilities no amount of practice can overcome.[19] This is why we consistently see Kenyans winning marathons and why Asians tend to be good at math. It's not just the existence of opportunities that creates success; it's the fact that there seem to be some things we were made to do and some things we were not.

How do we find such things? What makes some little boys and girls want to be athletes instead of musicians? Or what causes a painter to want to learn computer programming, for that matter? We can learn a lot from case studies of famous athletes and musicians and deepen our understanding of skill acquisition through research, but what science can't prove—what we still don't know— is what makes a person want to practice in the first place. What drives a person to put in those countless hours of practice?

Where does motivation *come* from? "It starts with a spark," Daniel Coyle told me in an interview. "You get a vision of your future self. You see someone you want to become. . . . It's a very mysterious process."[20]

—⚋—

When my son Aiden saw the animated Pixar movie *Cars* for the first time, he was transfixed. He had seen films and cartoons before but none that could hold his attention. *Cars* was different. At one year old, he watched the entire movie from start to finish without stopping, which he had never done before. Now he has enough merchandise from the movie to fill two entire bedrooms. He is obsessed. Neither my wife nor I pushed any of this on him, but the moment he saw the cars race across the screen, he lit up—and ever since, he's loved it.

Was there something innate in Aiden, something maybe even God-given, that made him love that movie? I don't know. That's not really the point. What I do know is that his attraction to a cartoon says something to me about my son: Aiden has a personality. And with that unique personality comes a destiny that is all his own, one independent of external circumstances and upbringing. Sure, his mom and I can influence him, and his friends can rub off on him, and his genes may dictate the extent of certain abilities, but that is not where his future ends. It's where it begins. There will always be those "spark" moments when who he is and what he is meant to be shine through.

No one illustrates this better than Garrett Rush-Miller, the boy whose handicap proposed severe limitations on his life. At five years old, he was blind and unable to walk, and the doctors were skeptical of how long he would live. And yet, the moment he touched that tandem bicycle, everything changed. He "lit up," according to his dad. That was his spark.

Our natural talent, or lack thereof, is not enough. Neither is practice. Some skills will seem to come naturally while others have to be developed. We can try a lot of things, but some we will do better than others, and some failures are not challenges to overcome but signs of what we shouldn't be doing. But what we must have before any of this is an initial spark, that moment of inspiration when we, too, light up. Which is something entirely different from luck.

As Jim Collins pointed out in *Great by Choice*, Bill Gates was not the only high school student in the 1970s with access to computers. And Tiger Woods wasn't the only kid whose dad played golf. So why did these men succeed in extraordinary ways when the same opportunities were available to others? They embraced their opportunity and then did something extraordinary with it. "Luck, good and bad," Collins wrote, "happens to everyone, whether we like it or not." But when we look at those who achieve extraordinary success, we see people "who recognize luck and seize it, leaders who grab luck events and make much more of them."[21]

What makes a person successful, then, is not the luck, but what he or she does with it. Opportunities come. The question is what will you do when they arrive? Successful people are just as "lucky" as the unsuccessful. The difference is they do something remarkable with their lucky moment while the rest of the world sits around, waiting for the next lucky streak to come.

In that sense, we all have opportunities—not necessarily to

become whatever we want, but to become *someone*, the person we were meant to be. It's one thing to chalk up successes to good fortune, especially when they belong to someone else, and quite another to recognize that we live in a world of opportunity and we all can do something with what we've been given. Practice is what tests your resolve, what forces you to hone your abilities long after the spark has faded. Are you committed to the craft, or will you quit when it gets too hard?

The ultimate goal of practice is to reach a state of what K. Anders Ericsson calls "eminent performance," when a person goes "beyond the knowledge of their teachers to make a unique innovative contribution to their domain."[22] We all want to do something that we are good at, that the world in some way recognizes, but the point of practice is never just about skill acquisition. It's about making a contribution to the world. Which is why when we are in the midst of pursuing our calling, we must not only ask if this is something that we are good at, but if it is something *good*. We need more than excellence to satisfy the deepest longings of our souls.

Which should raise the question: Is it, perhaps, possible to succeed at the wrong thing?

It is, indeed.

The Curious Case of William Hung

If you were to do a Google search for "American Idol rejects," you would instantly retrieve a list of names that will forever live in Internet infamy. Toward the top of that list sits, of course, Stephanie

Fisher, the awkward grad student who embarrassed herself in front of Victoria Beckham. But long before Stephanie took the stage for the seventh time in 2010, William Hung appeared during the third season of the show to do a rendition of Ricky Martin's "She Bangs."

"I want to make music my living," he told the cameras moments before appearing before the judges.

At five-foot-six, wearing a blue button-up shirt with pictures of assorted shoes on it and sporting an overbite, William didn't look like the kind of person destined for the spotlight. Not unlike Stephanie's, his performance was underwhelming to the judges, who tried to hide their laughter while he moved his hips and sang off-key.

"You can't sing, you can't dance, so what do you want me to say?" Simon asked.

"I already gave my best, and I have no regrets at all," William said, his response contrasting with the typical confrontational responses the judges were accustomed to receiving. Then he added with pride, "You know, I have no professional training of singing and dancing."

To which Simon responded, "No? Well, there's the surprise of the century."[23]

In the end, it didn't work out for William and he was sent home like so many others. But something strange happened after that. Long before "going viral" became the phenomenon it is today, William Hung's audition video started racking up thousands, and then millions, of views on YouTube. Instead of people laughing at him, they cheered. A fan set up a site in his honor, and in the first week it received more than four million hits. Within a month, that number had exceeded eight million.

William began receiving e-mails from people thanking him for his courage and example, which made the young man wonder if there was a career hiding somewhere in all this fame. That was around the time he was offered his first record contract.

At the time of his audition, William was a civil engineering student at the University of California, Berkeley. After his performance on *American Idol*, he won the hearts of fans everywhere, as well as the attention of the media. Koch Entertainment offered him a deal that resulted in his first album, *Inspiration*, a collection of cover songs that sold more than two hundred thousand copies, followed by two other less successful records.

In 2004, William left college to pursue a career in music, making appearances on the shows of David Letterman, Ellen DeGeneres, and Howard Stern. He even returned for a guest performance on *American Idol*, the same show from which he was rejected only months before. It was, in a way, poetic justice. He had turned defeat into triumph and spent the next few years performing all over the world, living off the fame won by a viral video on YouTube.

In spite of its success, the career of William Hung was controversial. Some criticized his fame, saying it reinforced Asian stereotypes and promoted racism, as he was thought to have no real musical talent. Others rooted for him. They loved his tenacity. None of the critiques seemed to bother the endlessly optimistic William, who knew how much his story meant to his fans. He was living his dream and sharing it with the world.

In 2011, though, that dream died when William ended his music career by accepting a job as a technical crime analyst.[24] Was he giving up on his dream? Weren't the millions of fans proof he had found his calling, that music was what he was supposed to be doing with his life? Maybe not. In an earlier interview, he told a reporter, "I may disappoint you with saying this, but I'm actually hoping to become a math teacher someday." In the same interview, he shared his love for the Pythagorean theorem and said that his favorite mathematician had to be Euclid.[25]

Sometimes it just takes a little time to find out what you are meant to do with your life. As I watched William light up while talking about math, it's no wonder he became an analyst whose daily responsibilities include calculating the probability of criminal activity.[26] In that earlier interview, he offered clues as to where his true passion lay, saying things like engineering "takes even greater dedication" than music.[27]

Does that really sound like someone who's destined to be a musician?

"My passion has always been math," he told a reporter after his almost decade-long stint with fame. "It just took a while to end up as my career."[28]

Through the long and windy road toward his calling, William learned about perseverance and staying true to his passion, in spite of what people say. In a speech delivered at a Toastmasters meeting, he said, "When you see a little hope, doors will open. . . . Never give up, because all you need is a little hope."[29]

Watching him retell his story one YouTube clip after another, I can see why so many people were fans of William. He knows he's being ironic. He knows he can't sing as well as Ricky Martin and that he's an awkward dancer, but that doesn't stop him from trying. He just loves music. And this, I think, is why we love William

Hung. He's an underdog. Yet, in spite of the accolades, fame and fortune were not enough to hold his attention. And therein lies a lesson for us all.

Success is a process of persevering through difficulties, but it's also about knowing yourself. What William might have added to that inspiring Toastmasters speech is that occasionally you step through the wrong door. You misapply the principles of practice and end up succeeding at the wrong thing or discovering your career is somehow a shadow of your true calling. Which is why we must think of this process as a journey. That was what Martyn Chamberlin discovered about his art. Though a passion, painting wasn't the end of the road for him; it was the beginning. In his case, being an artist opened a door to another skill he might never have encountered otherwise.

In any vocation, there comes a time when you realize the path you're on is not taking you where you want to go. All this preparation has culminated in helping you achieve the wrong goal. At those times, you might feel stuck. What do you do then? You do what William Hung finally did. You realize it's never too late to change and take a turn in the direction of your true calling.

PART TWO

Action

FOUR

Building Bridges

The Leap That Wasn't a Leap

Climate is what we expect. Weather is what we get.

—MARK TWAIN

Discovering your calling is not an epiphany but a series of intentional decisions. It looks less like a giant leap and more like building a bridge.

The day Myles Carlson was dropped off at a French-speaking school in the middle of East Africa was one of the hardest days in his mom's life. "I felt like I was tossing him into the sea without a life jacket," Kristy Carlson recalled. "Asking him to rise to the challenge of life in a new language just felt like too much to ask of a five-year-old!"[1] But Myles wasn't the only one who had to adjust to a new normal.

A few years before that day, Ben and Kristy Carlson knew they needed a change. The result was a "journey of discovery," as they called it, into who they were as individuals. For Kristy that meant pursuing photography, and for Ben it meant growing coffee. When they decided to go for it, moving from South Africa where they did leadership development and training with a Christian organization to become social entrepreneurs in Burundi, the Carlsons had no idea what to expect. They wanted to make a positive impact but didn't have a clue how to get started. Only after arriving in East Africa did they understand what would be required of them and how much bigger this move was than they imagined.

Before making the move, the family had zero exposure to the French language or Burundian culture, and both those facts hit them hard when they made the transition. Kristy wrote me, saying, "Ben and I joke that we've only been in Burundi for two and a half years, but it feels like ten because of the steep learning curve involved with our move." This was not what they had intended for their family when first moving to Africa a decade ago, and they were far from prepared. So what made them take the leap? In a word: *passion*.

"I can wake up, drink and talk about coffee all day long and not get tired," Ben Carlson said in a TV interview. "When I started realizing that, I started realizing that this was what I wanted to do. This was who I wanted to be."[2]

Watching this interview online after a friend referred it to me, I knew I needed to hear the Carlsons' story from their own mouths. So I reached out via e-mail and heard back from Kristy a week later. She apologized for the delay but explained that life can be pretty crazy in Burundi.

Once they had decided to pursue a change, she told me, the Carlsons searched for ways to pursue their passions. "Each pursuit led to more clarity," she said, "and acted as more preparation for a larger change . . . Even after we moved to Burundi, we weren't done changing. A year and a half after our move, we began our business. We did not feel that our destiny was something better or bigger than what we had been doing. Instead, we felt a desire to do work in the areas that we loved and craved a shift in those directions."

The Carlsons uprooted their family and moved to a remote part of the world because it was an opportunity to make a difference doing what they love. As it turns out, this is a great formula for moving in the direction of any calling: find what you love and what the world needs, then combine them. As Frederick Buechner wrote, "Vocation is the place where our deep gladness meets the world's deep need."[3]

When we think of someone pursuing a calling, we often picture a person who has it all together, someone who knows from the beginning what they were born to do. They have a plan. A person hears from God and becomes a priest. A professional athlete who grew up kicking a ball around the yard becomes a world-class soccer player. We picture someone who *just knew* what they were supposed to do with their lives and, at the right time, did it. But a calling doesn't always work like that. Sometimes, perhaps often, it is messy.

I asked Kristy how she and her husband knew this was the right decision—moving their family to one of the poorest countries in the world and starting a coffee company—and she admitted they didn't. "We were leaping," she said, "and it was a gangly, imperfect, headlong kind of leap at that. We felt strongly that it was time for a change, but our decision to incorporate Burundi into that change was based solely on the presence of an opportunity."

The operative word in that last sentence is *opportunity*. What the Carlsons were doing when they moved to Burundi wasn't just taking a blind leap of faith, nor was it executing a carefully crafted plan with precision. Just like the day they dropped off their son at school, it was a mix of both trust and intention.

The "You Just Know" Illusion

For the longest time, I believed a little lie about people who were fulfilling their purpose, and it prevented me from finding my own calling. What was it? One simple phrase: *you just know*. When we find someone doing what they love for a living, we tell ourselves a story. It's a nice piece of fiction, a familiar fairy tale, and a downright lie.

Here's how it goes. How did you know you wanted to be a fireman? What made you decide to go back to grad school? How did you know this was your calling? *I just knew.* This is what we hear from people who are too humble to admit how hard they worked or are uncomfortable with acknowledging how they got lucky. It sounds like how we often describe falling in love. *You just know.* The problem is that it isn't true.

Falling in love may be a mysterious process, but it is also an intentional one. He asked you out, you said yes, you kissed on the first date even though that was something you never did, and you started seeing each other exclusively. There is a process. And every single step of the way is marked by trust. This was what Eric Miller told me, what Jody Noland emphasized, and what Ginny Phang kept saying over and over—they all had no idea what they were doing. There was no plan. But they acted anyway. They didn't just know. They chose.

Maybe some people do *just know* what they're supposed to do with their lives. Maybe they're born with a sixth sense that allows them to intuitively understand they were meant to be a seamstress or a bullfighter, that they were born to make movies or build skyscrapers. But most people, the normal people you and I encounter on a daily basis, seem to have no clue. And telling these folks "you just know" when most of us clearly do not seems cruel.

We rarely hear this side of the story in interviews and documentaries about famous people. Why is this? Maybe because it sells. Because we'd rather believe the fairy tale that says some people are just special. That way, we don't have any responsibility to act.

This lack of honesty has produced a mythology in the world of work. The myth goes like this: Your calling, if it comes at all, is something that arrives one day on your doorstep in a neatly wrapped package. You don't have to worry about exerting any effort or anything; it will just work out. And if it doesn't, then it wasn't meant to be. Sorry, you must be doomed to dwell in a cubicle for the rest of your life, eking out a mediocre existence. At least you can live vicariously through those fortunate few who *do* get to find their callings.

Of course, we know this isn't true. We all want to believe we have the opportunity to find a life of meaning and purpose, to do work that matters. So why does such a life seem so evasive, and why is it so rare? Because we've believed in this myth that we will *just know* when it's time to commit. And that's hardly ever the case. Commitment is costly; it *should* scare us.

When I asked the Carlsons if what they were doing was the one thing they were born to do, Kristy said, "I think that we could do a multitude of things, but starting a business in Burundi that produces amazing coffee and helps the farmers who grow it incorporates both of our strengths and passions. Being coffee producers allows us to produce coffee of the highest quality while developing lasting relationships with coffee farmers. We might not be your usual suspects, and our journey has been full of ups and downs, but it is a beautiful thing to be sitting here typing in my office and overhearing our team talk passionately about ways to improve coffee farmers' lives."

The process of finding and claiming your calling is a journey, one that requires you to leave what you know in search of what you don't know. Yes, there's mystery to it, but the way you go about it is by putting one foot in front of the other. And when you are presented with an opportunity, you may not just know. But you will have to act. And that action is a little more complicated than we might think.

The Prophet Who Almost Missed His Call

Three thousand years ago, four or five miles northwest of Jerusalem in the hill country of Ephraim, there was a small town called Ramah, where a man named Elkanah lived. He had two wives, one who was infertile and the other who reminded her of this constantly.

Once during a trip to the ancient city of Shiloh, the barren wife Hannah was so plagued with shame that she made a public vow. If she would become pregnant, she would give her son to the high priest, dedicating his life to religious service. Shortly after, she conceived a son and named him Samuel. As soon as he was weaned, he was sent to Shiloh to serve the priest Eli.

Samuel was a special boy, a gift to his parents who long awaited his birth and a gift to Eli who only had disobedient sons. He served the priest in the work that he did, and the older man groomed him for a promising future.

One night, after months if not years of service, Samuel awoke before dawn. Startling awake, he sat up in bed and looked around. Nothing.

He swore he'd heard somebody whispering his name. But no one was there. Settling back into bed, the boy fell asleep only to be awakened again a few seconds later. This time, he was sure; it *was* a voice.

"Here I am!" he shouted back. No answer. Running into Eli's room, he shouted, "Here I am; you called me."

Eli rose out of bed, squinting his eyes, which were beginning to fail him.

"I did not call," he said, confused. "Go back and lie down."

Samuel was confused as well, but he did not want to argue with his master. So he returned to his room and slowly laid his head back down. He forced his eyes shut, too anxious to sleep. For what seemed like hours but in reality was only a few minutes, Samuel lay in bed. Then as his eyelids began to grow heavy, he heard it again, just as quiet as before but persistent as ever.

"Samuel . . ."

He shot up in bed, his heart racing. He called his master again while once again rushing into Eli's room. Again, the two were equally confused.

"My son," Eli said. "I did not call. Go back and lie down."

But before Samuel could even put his head down on the pillow, he heard the voice again, even louder than before. He got up again and called to Eli, his voice quivering with fear.

But the master's response was different this time. He told the boy to stop calling and instead to listen, giving him six words to say. So Samuel returned to bed and listened. When he heard the call a final time, he responded:

"Speak, for your servant is listening."[4]

After that, his life was never the same.

How the boy heard and answered his call led to many significant events in Israel's history, including the anointing of two kings, one who became the most famous the country would ever know. Samuel was called, and he answered. But the scary part—the part we should pay attention to—is that he almost missed it.

—⁓—

In the midst of your apprenticeship, perhaps while serving someone else's dream, you will make a discovery of your own. At first, it will come imperceptibly, like a whisper. But as you pay attention, it will greet you in forms you may not understand. It may come early in the morning or late at night, whenever you are still and the most vulnerable. Gently, it will speak to your heart, calling greatness out of you that you never knew existed.

We all hear such a call at some point, but many ignore it, discarding the voice as a dream. Some flee their calling their whole lives, avoiding that small persistent voice or staying busy enough to miss it. Many don't even take the time to listen in the first place. But the ones who do, those whose stories we remember, step out of hiding and say those six brave words: speak, for your servant is listening. It's as much an act of vulnerability as it is one of availability.

As children, we understand the world is a place that needs our gift, a place that is full of mystery and opportunity. We relish these facts. But as adults, we ignore such silly things; and for a time, it works. We go through life, focused on comfort and security and social stature, but as we continue ignoring the call that beckons our souls to awaken, we grow restless. And the voice grows louder until one day it is unbearable.

The story of Samuel is not a case for how calling comes—that voice sounds different to every ear. The point is that sometimes, we have to learn how to hear in the first place. If calling didn't come naturally to a young boy in ancient Israel, how much less will it come in today's busy world full of noise and interruption? We must listen. But we must also act. For the young boy who became a prophet, it was a trial-and-error process. He got the call wrong three times before he got it right.

It would be easy to hear this story and make the mistake of thinking calling starts with an epiphany. It doesn't. In fact, clarity of calling comes more through a series of deliberate decisions than it does through any sudden revelation. Looking at the story of Samuel, we see a boy going through his usual routine when he is interrupted by a strange incident that sets his life on a new course. This is how calling happens: not as a lightning bolt, but as a gentle, consistent prodding that won't leave you alone until you act. That you respond to the call, not how, is what makes it extraordinary.

In Samuel's case, he had a transcendent encounter, but at the time it felt ordinary. First, he misunderstood it. Then he asked for guidance—somewhat unwittingly, because he thought his master was calling him. Finally, he recognized the voice and submitted to it. It took some failure to get there, but he just took it one step at a time. When it comes to a call, that's all we can do. We can't control where or when it comes, but we can control who we are in those moments.

My own experience of discovering what I was meant to do was both powerful and ordinary. My friend Paul asked me what my dream was, and when I told him I didn't know, he said, "Really? I would've thought your dream was to be a writer."

"Yeah," I said. "I guess you're right. I'd like to be a writer— someday."

"Jeff," he said, looking me in the eyes, "you don't have to want to be a writer. You *are* a writer. You just need to write."

After that conversation, I began to write like never before. Every day at five a.m. for a year, I got up and wrote a few hundred words before sunrise. Without fail, I practiced. Why? Because I finally understood who I was. And once I grasped my identity, the activity followed.

Samuel didn't know God was speaking to him until his mentor Eli helped him understand what was happening. The boy, according to the story, was hearing from God and still needed help. The epiphany was not enough. The same was true for me with my conversation with Paul. Often our lives are speaking to us in extraordinary ways, but we lack the ability to hear or interpret the message. Understanding the signs, even hearing the actual call, can only take you so far. What must come next is a decision. And here is the point: finding your calling, as mysterious as it seems, is not only a mystical process; it is intensely practical. You either act on what you know, or you miss your moment.

The Stages of Discovery

Any great discovery, especially that of your life's work, is never a single moment. In fact, epiphany is an evolutionary process; it happens in stages.

First, you hear the call. It may sound different to each person, but it comes to us all. How we hear and respond to it is what matters. Sadly, many people never recognize the voice summoning them to greatness. Like Samuel, they hear something but aren't quite sure what to make of it. And without the aid of a mentor or guide, they're left to make sense of it on their own, which means they may get it wrong.

This is why apprenticeship is so important. Often, discovering what you're meant to do with your life doesn't happen until you have spent significant time serving someone else's dream. We learn what a calling looks like from mentors and predecessors before we can even begin to trust our own voice of calling. Only after you've put yourself in the shop of a master craftsman can you understand what your craft requires. Humility is a prerequisite for epiphany. Without it, your dream will be short-lived and self-centered.

Second, you respond. Mere words will not suffice—you must act. A true response to a call requires effort; you have to do something. In Samuel's case, he repeatedly got out of bed, going to see what his teacher wanted, in spite of the priest's protests that he was not calling him. What Samuel lacked in astuteness, he made up for with persistence. Apparently, that's all it takes. A little tenacity will get you to your calling.

Third, you begin to believe. This is the paradox of vocation. We think that passion comes first, that our desire is primary; but if we are truly called, the work always comes before we are ready. We will have to act in spite of feeling unprepared. "The gifts do not precede the call," someone once told me. And as we step into our life's work, we discover that we have been preparing for this our whole lives, even though in that very moment we feel insufficient. This is how you know you're called at all—the experience compels you to grow, to change.

A calling, though mysterious at times, requires a practical response. The way we make our way from dream to reality is through small intentional steps. Decisions reveal opportunity.

Samuel was more prepared than he realized. He had already moved and was living with a holy man, poised for epiphany. And quite by accident, he had done several things to make himself ready for the call, including finding a mentor. Of course, it wasn't his choice—his parents had done that for him—but in a way, that's the point. You will inherit opportunities that you didn't earn on your own, and if you are paying attention, you will recognize them for what they are—chances to hear the call.

The Carlsons' move to South Africa provided a similar setup for the call to Burundi. They didn't know this ahead of time, but that's the beauty. A calling takes everything you've done up to a certain point and turns it into preparation. Ben and Kristy were available, so when the opportunity arrived, they took it. For Ginny Phang, there was a nagging feeling in her gut that told her to not have the abortion. That was her setup. She didn't know where it came from or why it was there; she just knew she had to trust that feeling. "Even though my head did not know how to make it work . . . my heart felt so right," she said.[5]

Answering a call will sometimes feel that way. It won't make sense and may even open you up to rejection and criticism, but in your heart you will know it's right. How? There will be confirmation. You will take a step, and things will happen. Opportunities will reveal themselves. Through the words of others and even in the pit of your stomach, you will know this is the path to take—not because it is easy or safe, but because it is right.

This doesn't mean a calling is just an emotion, but feelings play a part in the process, and there comes a point when you can trust them. How do you know? You prepare. You put yourself in a place where you can hear the call, you have someone to help you discern the message, and then you make yourself available to act.

Feelings by themselves aren't entirely reliable, but we can test them against the wisdom of others. We can find a mentor, as Samuel did. We can put ourselves in a position of preparation, as the Carlsons did. Never were they guaranteed success, and rarely did they know what was coming next, but each step wasn't as final as it felt. Every decision opened up a new opportunity.

You might be thinking by now that your life is beginning to move in a direction. There may be momentum building behind your dream, and even the idea of a calling is starting to crystallize. Or maybe you feel as lost as ever. Regardless, remember this is still the beginning. Every step will reveal new choices to make.

Take time to look back at all you've experienced, and listen to what your life is saying. Invite mentors into your life to help you discern the call. This is the perfect opportunity to identify a thread, some common theme that ties everything together. As you begin to see the patterns, don't move too quickly. Just take one step at a time, trusting that opportunities will open at the right time.

The Worst Mistake You Can Make

My freshman year of college, I had a crush on a girl named Lane. With curly hair and a sweet smile, Lane was cute. She was also two years older than me. Since I had just broken up with my girlfriend, I was eager to get back in the game of dating, and Lane seemed to be the perfect girl.

When I told my friends I was going to ask her out, they asked how I was going to do it.

"I thought I'd just call her," I said.

"What?!" my friend Doug exclaimed. He was always the romantic. "Jeff, are you kidding me? You've got to sweep this girl off her feet. Go big or go home, man."

So I did what any college male with a guitar in the corner of his dorm room would do: I wrote Lane a song. At ninety seconds of pure lyrical delight, it was the essence of romance and took me only a few days to write.

One Saturday afternoon, I picked up the phone and called Lane's number. Three rings, and then a click.

"Hello?" a voice answered. It was her.

I slammed the phone against the receiver, grabbed my guitar, and stepped outside, shutting the door behind me. Because now I knew. Lane was home. Racing across campus with guitar strap slung over my shoulder, I ran to her dorm. Catching my breath in the lobby, I waited for someone to let me in, then walked straight to her door and knocked.

The door opened. And I stepped into a room full of people.

About half a dozen people were sitting around Lane's living room, chatting as college students tend to do on a Saturday afternoon. As soon as I entered the room, they all turned to me. Lane smiled nervously and looked at me. I didn't say a word.

Swinging the guitar from behind my back, I pulled it up to my chest and began to play. For the next one and a half minutes, I serenaded Lane, trying my best to ignore the onlookers. The song finished with the on-key line: "Will you go to the dance with me?" When I resolved with that final strum of the C chord, I looked at Lane, waiting for her answer.

She looked at me. I looked back at her. And everyone else looked at us.

And I waited.

Taking a deep breath, I grinned at her with fake confidence. This was the moment I had been waiting for, what I had been working up to for weeks now. I had, as my friends suggested, gone big, laying all my cards on the table. Now it was up to her.

Lane opened her mouth and let out two soul-crushing words: "I . . . can't."

My head dropped in defeat.

"I'm sorry."

Shoulders slumped, I nodded, pretending to understand. But then I did something even worse: I didn't leave. Instead of excusing myself, I sat down in the middle of the room and tried to blend in.

As if somehow that would be less embarrassing than just playing a song in front of a bunch of people, getting rejected by a girl, and then leaving.

I attempted to join the conversations, only to be greeted by looks of curiosity. But I played it cool: *What, that? That thing I just did? Oh, I do that every Saturday. In fact, I have three more gigs lined up today! This is just another stop on the College Dormitory Rejection Tour.*

Unable to bear the awkwardness any longer, I finally got up, walked across the room, and excused myself. Lane rushed to the door to see me out, walking with me through the hallway. "Well, thanks for my song!" she said sweetly.

Through gritted teeth, I mustered in the most sarcastic voice possible, "Oh, my *pleasure*. I aim to entertain." And I left.

After that incident, it would be a long time before I would ever do something so audacious for a girl again. But looking back now, I understand how it happened the way it did. Why did Lane shut me down? Probably because I had uttered a total of one hundred words to her in the previous year we had known each other. In my mind, I had built up the fantasy of a relationship without ever sharing the vision with her.

I think we do the same thing with our dreams. First, we flirt with them from afar. Then we fantasize, imagining what life will be like when we are united with what we love, without ever doing any real work. We wait, building up courage, and save all our passion for the big day when we will abandon everything and go for it. And finally, we take the leap.

Sometimes, though, we don't make it to the other side. We fall on our faces. Doing our best to pick ourselves up, we dust ourselves off and try again. But if this happens enough, we begin to tell ourselves a familiar story. We remind ourselves that the world is a cold, cruel place, and maybe there's no room in it for *my dream*. We get disillusioned and make the worst mistake you can make with a calling: we save all our energy for the leap instead of building a bridge.

The problem with how we chase our passions is that reality doesn't always conform to how things appear in our minds. Lane said no because she didn't know me. And as much as I would have liked to think differently, I didn't really know her. Relationships take time, as do dreams. They're full of routines and unexciting work that make them unfit for a movie script but appropriate for real life. For nearly a decade, I did this with my passion. I dreamed of it, talked about it, even made "plans" for when luck would come my way and I'd be able to do what I love for a living. All along, though, I was kidding myself, believing the myth of the leap, which was the very thing holding me back from my dream.

The Truth About the Leap

In the 1930s, Belgian settlers started planting coffee in Burundi. For decades, the country was used to produce nothing more than commodity coffee, its natural resources neglected and depleted.[6] Although it contained a vast supply of rich resources, Burundi's coffee was overlooked. That is, until recently.

If you take a look at a chart of the world's poorest countries, you will see Burundi almost at the top of the list, with the second lowest GDP in the world.[7] Farmers in Burundi plant all kinds of crops—bananas, cassava, and beans—but coffee is one of their only cash crops, accounting for 80 percent of the country's export revenues. More than half the population makes its living from coffee.[8] Coffee pays for farmers' school fees for their kids, medical bills for their families, and whatever food they can't grow themselves. In Burundi, coffee is a matter of life and death.

Apparently, when grown and roasted just right, Burundian coffee is a drinking experience unlike no other African bean. Due to poor distribution, however, much of the coffee-drinking world has been missing out on this. Burundian coffee doesn't get the attention it deserves, and Ben and Kristy Carlson intend to change that. For them, coffee is not just a passion to be pursued. It's a chance to make a difference in the lives of a community, if not an entire country. They started with a washing station for the coffee, but as time went on, they formalized the project.

The birth of Long Miles Coffee Project was not only a way for Ben and Kristy to get involved in the coffee business; it was an opportunity to offer hope. Nearly two-thirds of the Burundi population lives at or below the poverty line,[9] and due to a lack of infrastructure, middlemen take most of the revenues from coffee production.[10] The goal of the project is to improve the lives of local farmers through direct trade, helping them get better wages.

These farmers are not some far-off cause to which the Carlsons send money every month. They are their neighbors. They see these people every day; their kids play together. Because they work in one of the poorest countries on the planet, it's important to them to not only understand the people they're trying to help, but to experience life with them.

When they first entertained moving to Burundi, Ben and Kristy couldn't comprehend the implications of their dream and never would have anticipated all the battles they would face while building a business in the developing world. But they knew they had to find a way, and that determination led to wisdom. They studied and planned and prayed, and when they didn't know what to do, they took a leap. But in that "leap," there is a lot to unpack.

The Carlsons didn't just decide to move anywhere. They researched the industry and found an opportunity to help producers get high-quality coffee to an exploding global market.[11] And they made their move on far less of a whim than we might think, spending a decade in South Africa before making the transition. Sure, it was still an adjustment to learn French and acclimate to another culture, but calling it a "leap" isn't quite right. If anything, they built a bridge.

Ben and Kristy were able to do all this because they understood the *why* behind what they were doing. They had a reason that went beyond themselves and their own comfort. This wasn't just about them—it was about the difference they wanted to make. So when doubt crept into their minds, they didn't get stuck or stop. They found a way. Instead of waiting for the perfect path to be revealed, they saw an opportunity and took it. They started, knowing that flexibility would be essential—but they also weren't foolish in how they made the transition.

Even now, two and a half years later, there are challenges and cultural differences that frustrate them. Realizing the purpose behind the work they do, though, and that they're a part of something bigger than themselves, has made it worth all the trouble. They didn't take a leap; they built a bridge. And the beauty of a bridge is you don't have to see too far ahead in order to get to the other side. You just have to take the next step.

Not Knowing Is No Excuse

A couple of years ago, my friend Bryan Allain left a secure job at a Fortune 500 company, where he'd been slowly climbing the corporate ladder for nearly a decade, to venture out on his own as a writer.[12] When I asked him how his colleagues reacted, he said they were surprisingly supportive, some even envious. But something disturbed him.

Every conversation ended the same way. "I wish I could do that," they would say. "Well, you can, you know," Bryan would respond. To which they would usually list out the reasons why they felt they couldn't. They wouldn't know where to begin or what to do. They'd be scared of losing their health benefits or risking their family's well-being. *What if you failed*, they wondered. *What then?* This bothered Bryan because he felt like what they were really saying was that they were afraid—and rightly so. Quitting a job to chase a dream is anything but safe. If you're not feeling a little insecure about taking such a leap, then you probably haven't considered the cost. The problem, then, isn't the fear; that's natural. It's that many get afraid and stay there.

We all deal with this fear on some level. What fills us with anxiety, if we let it, is a simple phrase that keeps us from our purpose. It's six simple words: "I don't know what to do." What should I write about? What kind of music should I play? What type of business do I open? Where do I begin? I don't know. And with that seemingly innocuous response, a dream can die. But what we're really saying in these moments of not knowing is that we want the journey to be safe. We want it drawn out for us—no surprises or setbacks, just a clear beginning and end. Unfortunately, that's not the way the process usually works.

One way to think of it is in terms of maps and globes. Maps are easy. They're flat and predictable, easy to chart out a course. You can see the whole landscape in a simple, two-dimensional layout. However, as easy as they are, maps are unrealistic. The world isn't flat; it's not color coded and foldable and easily stored in your car's glove box. Life is too complex and beautiful to be captured on a map. It may help you see the big picture, but it does not help you understand the magnitude of the journey.

A globe, on the other hand, is complex. It spins on an axis. Some globes are even topographical, raised in certain areas where there are mountains or major bodies of water. They're not the easiest tools in the world to use and certainly more difficult to store, but they're just about the best picture we have of reality. Typically, you use a map to travel from one state or province to the next, usually a relatively short distance, whereas you use a globe to travel the world.

Which would you rather use, a map or a globe? It depends on where you're going.

When people asked Bryan the specifics of how he would pursue his dream, he was honest, admitting he didn't know all the answers. He didn't have a map. He wasn't even sure exactly where he was headed; all he cared about was moving forward. Here's how he once described it to me in conversation: "Say you live in Kansas. It's not a bad place to live, but you long for the beach. You dream of the waves and sand and sunsets. But you never leave home because you're not quite sure exactly where on the beach you want to go."

If you aren't sure how to get started, Bryan would say get out of Kansas. That's your first step. Begin to head toward water, and as you move, you'll find the beach. Once you're there, you can pick whatever spot you like. You don't need a specific address to begin. The path to your dream is more about following a direction than arriving at a destination.

When you start pursuing your calling, you may find it to be more difficult than you thought it would be. And that's okay. It means the journey is bigger than you expected. What you must do is keep moving. Don't stand still. Don't squander your time, holding out for someone else to give you permission to start. It won't happen that way. No one is going to give you a map. You will have to step out into the unknown, listening for direction as you go. And when you are in doubt, just remember to drive toward water. You can always change directions once you get in the car.

Anyone Can Do This

A year and a half after moving to Burundi, the Carlsons turned their dream into a business. They wanted to help as many people as possible, and they saw the potential for Long Miles Coffee to be something significant. They went all in.

Committed to providing fair prices to farmers and inspired by Benjamin Zander's words that "money follows contribution,"[13] they decided to make a go for it with the business. They didn't know everything before taking that step, but they trusted that things would come together. "I'm not saying everyone should run out and quit their jobs," Kristy wrote me. "I am saying that some risks are worth taking and that as we take them, opportunities often open up." And so far, it has worked out.

At times, Ben and Kristy both feel like quitting. They are open about this, even sharing such doubts on their blog. This is what makes them so likable. They seem like ordinary people (because they are). Even after making the "leap," they still don't have perfect clarity. Doing what they're meant to do, at times, is messy. When the power is out for the eleventh day straight or a family member gets sick, Kristy says she wishes she could be back home in the United States, where high-quality health care and electricity are a given. "Burundi will always be a difficult place for me to live," she said. "It is rich and full, but difficult."

Rich and full, but difficult. These same words could be used to describe a calling. From Garrett Rush-Miller, the five-year-old with a brain tumor, to Ginny Phang, the woman whose family disowned her because she didn't have an abortion, this is a constant theme. Finding your life's work is not easy. It may, in fact, cause you more pain than comfort, but it will be worth the cost. In spite of the difficulties they face, the Carlsons can't help but hope. As their team grows, they feel themselves being strengthened daily.

Such is the reality for any journey of vocation. If your life's work is only a dream, something fleeting and frail that's never backed by action, it can only last so long. When difficulties come, and they always do, you will be inclined to give up and move on to something easier. But if your calling is more than a good idea and you're willing to put in the hard work and persevere, taking bold steps along the way, you can stand firm in the face of hardship.

At one point during our interview process, I made the mistake of suggesting the Carlsons made the leap due to a sense of being called to something great, which Kristy quickly corrected: "We were hoping that the impact we would make was a positive one," she said, "but we didn't and don't believe that we are called to do something greater than anyone else is. We believed we were called to bring our skills to the table of life, to look for opportunities where we could contribute in the world. I think placing words like 'greatness' near us makes it seem as if we are not your average human being, and we really are. Any person could move in the direction that we did if it seemed like the right fit for them, even if it's just one small step at a time."

FIVE

Pivot Points

Why Failure Is Your Friend

If at first you don't succeed, try, try
again. Then quit. There's no point
in being a damn fool about it.

—W. C. FIELDS

*It will take a few tries before you get your
calling right. Failure isn't what prevents us
from success, then. It's what leads us there.*

Matt McWilliams always assumed he would grow up to
become a golf pro. Born just five hundred yards from the
second green of Pinehurst No. 2, a North Carolina resort known
as "The Cradle of American Golf," he thought it was his destiny
to follow in his father's footsteps. What he never could have imagined, though, was that his own dad would have to fire him, and he
would continue to face rejection for the next several years—all of
which would somehow lead to his calling.[1]

In high school, Matt won four out of five major junior golf tour-
naments in Tennessee, including the Tennessee State High School
championship. In college, he won the Adams Cup of Newport, the
Berry College Spring Invitational, the Carolinas Amateur, and others. He was the number-one player at the University of Tennessee
and was so confident that golf was where his future lay that he
didn't bother to graduate.

Matt went on to play professional golf for a year until one day when an acute pain in his wrist that started in college began to worsen. The pain crept all the way up the left side of his body and eventually became so crippling that he was forced to see a doctor. Diagnosed with acute tendonitis, he was told he could either undergo serious surgery or cut back on golf. He opted for the latter. That's when he decided he didn't want to play the game as badly as he thought he did. But what else could he do? Golf was all he had ever known, all he had ever expected, and all he had ever wanted. And now, unexpectedly, the plan was changing.

In the pursuit of our life's work, we will encounter obstacles and challenges that we think are a disruption to the course, something to overcome. But in fact, these very obstacles are sometimes the means to success. With nowhere to turn, Matt went to work for his dad at Knollwood Fairways in Southern Pines, North Carolina. Working at the course as an instructor, he discovered a new skill: online marketing. Most nights he would stay up late, building websites and advertising campaigns for golf classes that, ironically, he had no desire to teach. He had absolutely no interest in the business he was helping build. But the marketing? He loved that part, something he never would have learned if everything had gone according to plan.

Realizing he had a knack for attracting new clients, Matt started his own company, Fast Lane Consulting, as a side project in 2002 while still working at the golf course. But on July 1, 2003, a date Matt remembers because it was the day after his birthday, the unexpected happened. His dad let him go. The timing wasn't great, but he knew it had been coming. "It should have happened a lot sooner," Matt admitted. That was the *first* time he got fired.

During the summer of 2004, Matt spent half his time working with a congressional political campaign in North Carolina and the other half doing online marketing for consulting clients. This was a time when he continued to hone his online marketing skills, further falling in love with how words and images could motivate people. "I could spend thirty-six hours straight designing a website without any sleep," he recalled.

By the end of the campaign, Matt's clients no longer needed his services. Once again, he was about to face unemployment, and he didn't have a plan for what would come next. Running out of cash and living at home, he was relieved when a friend called, asking him to design an insurance website. It was just the kind of project he had been praying for, and it came at just the right time. But it was only one gig, and Matt needed more stability as he was getting older and wondering what he would do with the rest of his life.

Shortly after that project was completed, the friend called again, this time inviting Matt to help him start a new company, one that would generate sales leads for insurance companies. At first, Matt said no. He liked working for himself and enjoyed the freedom of being his own boss. But the friend asked again, and he still said no. By this time, though, things were starting to look desperate. With the business slowing down, he had fewer and fewer options, so he finally succumbed to his friend's offer.

In December 2004, they went into business together. The first thing they did was hire a programmer. Matt did all the sales, affiliate management, and web design. He learned about sales and marketing, even how to do some basic programming. The days were long and the work was exhausting, but he loved it.

By December 2007, the company had grown to forty employees and more than twelve million dollars in annual revenue. The company, based in Franklin, Tennessee, eventually grew to nearly twenty million dollars, won several awards, and was thriving in almost every respect—except when it came to relationships.

Matt was on top of the world. This was his dream job. At least, that's what he thought. But as his success grew, so did his ego. Notorious around the office for being a perfectionist and someone who would tear into you for the slightest infraction, Matt was a person you didn't want to be caught alone with in a hallway. You never knew what he might say.

One day, the two owners approached him, and as nicely as they could, they asked Matt to leave. He had been treating people poorly, and without knowing or caring, he was leaving a lot of "carnage" around the office, which they had to clean up. That was the second time Matt was fired. He was twenty-seven years old, and it happened just fifteen days before his wedding.

Taking six months off to enjoy his marriage and embark on what he calls "a spiritual journey," Matt went back to work in May 2009, joining a company in Nashville that sold instructional DVDs. The next year, he won the Affiliate Manager of the Year award at Affiliate Summit and ended up leading all their online marketing after that. The job lasted two years. During his second year, Matt had a nagging thought about starting his own consulting business and brought it up to his boss, who gave his blessing and even offered Matt some advice.

In February 2011, he left the company to return to his first job, the same place from which he had been fired two and a half years earlier. But his second stint was even shorter than the first. One Friday night during dinner, after he had been working there for nine months, Matt was complaining to his wife about the job, which had become a usual occurrence. His wife, who'd finally had enough, said he needed to decide *when* he was going to quit, which he agreed to and told her when he went into the office the next day he would set a date to leave. The next day, a private detective showed up at the McWilliamses' front door and said, "I'm here to collect your work laptop." That's how Matt found out he was laid off, and that was the day he decided to expand his part-time consulting business into a full-time endeavor.

Now Matt lives in Fort Wayne, Indiana, but his business is wherever his clients are: San Francisco, Boston, New York, Chicago, Washington. His story is not the typical tale of a little boy who always knew what he was going to do with his life and after overcoming insurmountable obstacles, finally persevered to find his dream. His journey is like a lot of ours, full of failure and unexpected mishaps, frustrating moments that make you question what you're doing. For those familiar with the confusion of not knowing if you're pursuing the right thing, Matt McWilliams's story offers a subtle encouragement: there's room to get your calling wrong.

And through all the twists and turns, after repeated rejection, something beautiful emerged: Matt found his calling. Not in the way you would expect, of course, but by now we should be expecting that. He didn't come to his life's work by success. He found it through failure.

The Power of the Pivot

In basketball, you are only allowed to take two steps once you stop dribbling the ball. When you take that last step, the foot you land on becomes what's called a "pivot foot." That foot must remain fixed, but the other foot can freely move about, allowing you to easily spin around and find a teammate to whom you can pass the ball. You can even pivot before dribbling the ball, allowing you to change direction before moving down the court. Although you are confined to where you are and how many steps you can take, at no point are you locked into any direction. That's the beauty of the move. Even when all other opportunities are exhausted, you can always pivot.

In 2006, Andrew Mason was about to attempt something big. A graduate student pursuing a public policy degree at the University of Chicago, he was doing some contract work on the side, building databases at a company founded by an entrepreneur named Eric Lefkofsky. In 2007, backed by Lefkofsky, Mason launched a company called The Point, a website intended to bring groups of people together to solve problems. The idea was that a person could use social media to get people to rally together around a specific cause and then motivate them to act. Nobody cared much about making money; it was about making a difference.

The start-up, in spite of its good intentions, didn't take off. To make matters worse, when the recession hit in 2008, they needed money, and without a business model The Point was in trouble. Normally the team would use the website to organize people around a cause, but this time they wanted to try something new, at the prodding of Lefkofsky. What if their cause this time was to *save* money?

The new idea, born out of financial distress, was to get twenty people to buy the same product and try to get a group discount. Although this concept had been introduced in the original business plan, when Lefkofsky brought it up again more than a year later, Mason and the other team members shot it down. This time, Lefkofksy wouldn't let it go. When the economy continued to spiral downward in late 2008 and the company was forced to lay people off, they knew it was time for a change.[2] "There was this pressure from the market crash [and] looking at our burn rate and revenue—it was time for us to try something to scratch that itch," a source from the company told Business Insider.[3]

And that's how Groupon, a company valued at almost thirteen billion dollars at the time of its IPO in 2011, was born.[4] How did they do it? They certainly didn't plan for any of it at the start. They did something much more effective. They pursued a strategy that has served entrepreneurs well since the dawn of business. They pivoted.

A pivot is powerful because it takes away all of your excuses. It puts you back in control of the game you're playing. Pivoting isn't plan B; it's part of the process. Unexpected things will happen; setbacks do occur. Whether or not you're prepared to pivot will affect how well you weather those storms and find a way to survive.

We often look at successful people, hearing their stories of failure, and think that they succeeded despite the fact that they failed. But that's not true. Successful people and organizations don't succeed *in spite* of failure; they succeed *because* of it. In the case of

Groupon, a failed philanthropy effort led to a for-profit enterprise that succeeded in ways the original founders never imagined. Sometimes failure is the best thing that can happen to you if you learn to listen to the lessons in it.

The world can be cruel. It's nobody's responsibility to make your dream come true. Tough times will come, and what determines a person's success during such trying times is the ability to pivot. Every calling encounters setbacks, and sometimes people don't want what you have to offer, or maybe they just don't understand it. Other times, life throws a curveball or the passion you once had wanes. At times like these, we are inclined to give up, but these are the moments that require our most intentional action.

In any pursuit, the temptation is to go it alone—to subscribe to a few blogs, read a business book, and start acting like an expert. We praise such entrepreneurial initiative, thinking it's what drives modern innovation, but we couldn't be more wrong. Every great endeavor begins with a smaller, less significant one. This is the season of failure that marks critical preparation steps of history's heroes. Albert Einstein worked in a patent office; Benjamin Franklin was forced to flee his hometown; Steve Jobs got kicked out of his own company. We all face times of irrelevance; of falling on our faces and thinking we have no business doing any of this. But pain is the great teacher and failure a faithful mentor. You can use all of this to your benefit if you are willing.

Einstein used his menial job to conduct "thought experiments." Franklin took his rejection and learned from it, trying to better understand people and later using what he learned as a diplomat, turning every shortcoming into strength. Jobs practiced playing

CEO at Pixar, a smaller company where it was easier to fail, before returning to Apple to bring it back to life. Failure is the best friend you will ever have if you learn from it. As Robert Greene wrote in his book *Mastery*, "Repeated failure will toughen your spirit and show you with absolute clarity how things must be done."[5]

How did Matt McWilliams turn his failure into success? He certainly didn't know where he was headed—there *was* no plan. When facing failure, Matt was realistic. He didn't accept defeat, but neither did he try to push through the doors that had closed. Instead, he did something creative. Just as Andrew Mason did, he pivoted, turning in a new direction and eventually finding his way.

A Season of Failure

Contrary to popular belief, Sam Adams never made beer. Beyond the Boston lager that bears his name, the world has largely forgotten who this man was, but to the Founding Fathers of the United States, he was an important and influential figure—and a man well acquainted with failure.[6]

A portly man who led a nation and its leaders with words, Adams roused a multitude to action through his numerous newspaper opinion articles and speeches. He was, in the words of Thomas Jefferson, "truly the Man of the Revolution." His second cousin John called him "zealous, ardent and keen in the Cause."[7] But before he commanded the respect of some of America's greatest heroes, he spent a good part of his life pivoting from one failure to the next.

First he tried to be a lawyer, and when that didn't work, he tried to be a maltster, a person who makes the malt that is later used to make beer. Later he tried his hand at business and failed at that too. No matter what he tried, success seemed to evade Samuel, and his family, who had high hopes for him, was beginning to worry he might not amount to much. It wasn't until he became involved in politics—initially through writing and attending town hall meetings—that he came alive, finding the thing he was born to do.

Through his writings, he became the voice of the American Revolution, and it was that voice that roused others like George Washington, Thomas Jefferson, and John Adams to the cause. After the war, he remained in politics but never became president. He was content with a governorship of his home state, Massachusetts, where he lived out the remainder of his days.[8] Were it not for his tenacity, his willingness to keep trying things until he found the right path, Samuel Adams never would have found his purpose, and a nation may have never been born.

Every calling is marked by a season of insignificance, a period when nothing seems to make sense. This is a time of wandering in the wilderness, when you feel alone and misunderstood. To the outsider, such a time looks like failure, as if you are grasping at air or simply wasting time. But the reality is this is the most important experience a person can have if they make the most of it.

As many do, you may be wondering what you're supposed to do with your life. Everything seems confusing and overwhelming. Your parents told you one thing, while your peers say something different. Who do you trust? Where do you focus? Traditional advice says to have a plan, but as we have seen, plans don't always work. When pursuing your life's work, your calling can be hard to see. Sometimes it has to be revealed, and the way this often happens is through failure.

When Matt McWilliams told me his story, I heard pieces of my own journey. I recalled those seven years of working for a nonprofit and the previous year of travel. I never felt like I had found my place but had a nagging suspicion that I was headed somewhere. By the end of the conversation, we both learned something. When we feel farthest from our purpose, we are actually already on the path, headed in the right direction. This means that when you are confused and failing, when all seems lost and you are just about to give up, you are closer to your destiny than you realize. The message of the pivot is that what looks like failure now is preparation for what's to come, as long as you don't give up.

So what separates a season of failure from a lifetime of failure? First you must be willing to recognize hardship as an opportunity to learn, willing yourself to push through failure. Second, you must be careful to not succeed at the wrong things. You have to pay attention to passion and beware of the temptation of success. It's not enough to be good at something; you must focus on what you are meant to do. And appreciate that your understanding of that, over time, just might change. So be ready to make more pivots along the way.

This was what Mother Teresa learned when beginning her ministry. After spending twenty years as a nun and schoolteacher, she faced a crisis that would force her to reevaluate everything. While riding on the train, she felt suddenly compelled to serve the poor—to not only give to the impoverished but also identify with them and become a part of their community. Trading her habit for a sari, she started the Missionaries of Charity, a new order that focused on this mission. It was a bold move and one that would take years of discernment before becoming a reality, but it was a vision she was certain of, something she could not avoid doing. She called this moment of inspiration a "call within a call." And what this means is that your vocation can evolve.[9]

Early in life, we start out on a certain path. As life continues, we settle down and have kids and maybe get a little wiser and find ourselves questioning earlier motivations and actions. We wonder if we were just foolish or idealistic. Equipped with a better understanding of the world, we now see things more clearly. We grow up. We may drift into complacency on occasion, but life also tends to stabilize and we make better decisions. So it makes sense that as we continue to grow, our understanding of calling will grow and expand and even change too.

A calling is not merely a moment; it's a lifestyle, a constant progression of submitting to a larger purpose. When you are first called, whether it comes as a whisper or a roar, what you hear is only part of the big picture, a shadow of something bigger. And as you move toward your life's work, you must deepen that awareness, looking for signs to hone your understanding and for opportunities to change direction along the way.

This is good news, because it means we can fail; we can miss the mark without veering completely off course. We can change directions and try new things, learning as we go. Your life's work is not a single event, but a process you are constantly perfecting, finding new ways to put your passion to work. And you do that one pivot at a time.

Life Is Not a Dream

A while ago, I called my friend Jonathan for some advice. He had started a publishing company, which was a dream of his for a number of years, and I wanted to know more about how that happened. What led to Jonathan's transformation in perspective, turning him from a dreamer into a doer? At first he was reluctant to share, but I kept prodding until he caved. Finally he said what changed for him was one simple phrase. Everything began to change after that, all thanks to a small but significant shift in vocabulary.

Every week Jonathan and his friends would get together for dinner, gathering around the kitchen table to talk about their hopes and dreams and what they would do with their lives *someday*.

"One night," he recalled, "we were all sitting around my kitchen table, talking like we always did. We were thinking about what life would be like when our dreams came true, if only circumstances were different, you know? And then someone spoke up and said, 'What if we stopped saying *what if* and started saying *let's*?'"

That was it for Jonathan. It was the challenge he needed to get started with his dream. Instead of saying "what if," he started saying "let's." He ditched the dreams and instead became a person of action. When I spoke with him on the phone, I could te' something had changed; he was a new man. It was a small shif minor pivot—but it made all the difference.

The lesson is clear. We can spend our days dreaming of a better life or do the messy work of getting started today. You are not just waiting on your calling; your calling is waiting on you. And you can sit around, playing the what-if game until you're exhausted, or you can begin by saying that one little word that changes everything: *let's*.

In the Spanish play *Life Is a Dream* by Pedro Calderón de la Barca, the protagonist, Segismundo, has been locked up in a tower for most of his life and delivers a monologue in which he describes life as nothing more than a dream. He says, "What is life? A tale that is told; / What is life? A frenzy extreme, / A shadow of things that seem; / And the greatest good is but small, / That all life is a dream to all, / And that dreams themselves are a dream."[10]

It's a profound and poetic monologue, the most famous in the play, but it's also a little depressing. What Segismundo is saying is that life itself is a fantasy and what we think we know is an illusion. This, unfortunately, is how many live their lives. Thinking of a calling as nothing more than an unrealized dream, they squander their passion and rob the world of a gift—their action. At the end of their lives, as their story fades into eternity, they will wonder, *Was it worth it? Did I do all I had to do? Or did I play it safe?*

On our deathbeds, we will see things with the most clarity we have ever had. Each of us will have to face the facts of how we spent our lives, especially when we had the opportunity to act and didn't.

n anything about that day is how I will have

times I didn't live up to my potential, why I

lling more fully. And what will my reason be?

el it. It's a force that afflicts even the most

courageous. So what do we do about it? We lean in, realizing that failure is inevitable, but it's also not a legitimate obstacle. We can keep moving, albeit sometimes in a different direction.

This is where your story starts to matter, when you begin to make a difference with the talents and skills you've acquired. It's where ideas and action meet; where we stop dreaming and start living. There is tension here in this place of action, and risk is inevitable. But the rewards are great. What we do with this moment will carry on for eternity. What you leave behind for posterity isn't a decision you make on your deathbed. It's a choice that happens right now with the resources available at this very moment.

There is, of course, an alternative. We could opt out, becoming bitter about the whole thing. We could believe this process of pursuing a passion is a farce. Like Segismundo, we could even get so lost in our own dream worlds that we aren't sure what is real. Certainly that's an option. The problem, though, is that nobody gets changed by an ideal; nothing gets shaken by a dream. And the world remains the same, regardless of how great your idea is. It's only when people take action that true transformation happens. Don't get me wrong. Dreams are powerful. They are fuel for change. But by themselves, they do no good. Hanging out in coffee shops and talking about one day being a writer or an activist or an entrepreneur is just about the worst thing you can do. It feels like work but is in fact destructive to the real work of realizing your dream.

So what do you do? Stop talking and start doing. Don't dream of being a writer—begin writing. Don't dream of being an activist—go start something. Don't dream of being an entrepreneur—launch something.

I recently caught up with Jonathan. He started that publishing company and ran it for several years, but as life moved on, his passion steered him in a new direction. So he ended the business and started something else, and as it turns out, the publishing company was just one more step in the journey. Had he never begun, he would never have ended up where he is today. The point isn't that he succeeded. He would say he didn't, not with the publishing company anyway. The point is he tried. He didn't stay stuck in the dream and instead adopted an attitude of doing. Anything less than such proactivity is a cheap imitation of the life you were meant to live. It's stalling. Instead of letting it stop you in your tracks, why not do what Jonathan did and pivot in a new direction? You might be surprised by the opportunities that present themselves.

The Hidden Message of Failure

Not all pivots have happy endings. In 1939, German pastor Dietrich Bonhoeffer set sail for America, a trip that marked a crucial turning point in his life. If he went in one direction, he might surely die. If he went in the other, he would never be able to live with himself.

A year earlier, thanks to his brother-in-law, he had met the members of the German Resistance, an underground group whose primary goal was to drum up support for a military-led coup against Hitler. From this meeting, he learned that the world was on the brink of war and that Germany's chancellor was more dangerous than most realized.

A committed pacifist outspoken against the Nazis, Bonhoeffer would never enlist in military service. At the same time, he knew not doing so might create complications for the church, as it would be viewed as an official stance. Unsure of what to do, he left for the United States, invited by Union Theological Seminary in New York.

Shortly after arriving, he regretted his decision. Some knew the danger he was in and the tough position he faced, so they urged him to stay. But he refused.[11]

In a letter to his friend Reinhold Niebuhr, Bonhoeffer described the two choices he had—stay in America and live, or go back to Germany and possibly be killed. He wrote, "I know which of these alternatives I must choose but I cannot make that choice from security."[12] He returned to Germany, where he was eventually harassed, detained, and executed for a plot to assassinate Hitler. He was hanged at Flossenburg concentration camp, just two weeks before American soldiers arrived to liberate the camp.[13]

The decision Bonhoeffer made in New York didn't lead to success. It didn't make him rich or famous. But it was the only decision he could make, one that agreed with his conscience, and a crucial turning point in his life. That one decision cost him his life. As he wrote in a letter a few years earlier, "My calling is quite clear to me. What God will make of it I do not know . . . I must follow the path. Perhaps it will not be such a long one."[14] Sometimes a calling isn't a means to a more comfortable life. Sometimes we don't pivot in the direction of personal success but toward even greater pain. But here's the catch: a calling will always lead you to a life that matters, one you can be proud of. The way that we get there, though, isn't always up to us. Sometimes the path can be costly, even deadly. But what lies at the end of the road is a prize that money can't buy and a legacy the world won't forget.

"It was the second best thing that ever happened to me," Matt McWilliams told me of the first time he was fired by his friends. The best was the second time they fired him, forcing him on a journey filled with unexpected twists and turns that ultimately led to his life's work. It was, at times, difficult, even painful, but the pain was worth the reward.

SIX

The Portfolio Life

A New Kind of Mastery

The future belongs to those who learn more
skills and combine them in creative ways.

—Robert Greene

*Your calling is not just one thing; it's a few
things. The trick is to not be a jack-of-all-
trades but to become a master of some.*

I n college, Jody Maberry studied finance and marketing. Anxious
to leave school and get into the business world, he looked forward to the day he could start wearing a shirt and tie every day.
But during his last year of school at Illinois State University, he
discovered their Outdoor Adventure program. He began taking
classes and trips with the department, and one trip in particular
to Yellowstone National Park left an impression on him. "I can't
tell you how cold it got in Yellowstone," he recalled, "because my
thermometer broke at twenty below. It was miserable and wonderful. When I returned, it was all I could think about."[1]

After graduating from ISU, Jody took to the road. He believed
he would end up living and working the rest of his life in central
Illinois, but due to the Yellowstone incident and the mark it left on
him, he was determined to see what else was out there. For three
months, he lived out of a tent and explored the western United States,

eventually making his way to Washington State. There he realized it's not always voices that call us to our life's work. Sometimes it's places. "Tossing rocks into the water at Deception Pass State Park," he wrote me in an e-mail, "I realized I could never go home."

Several weeks later, Jody did return home only to realize what he felt during his trip was not going to pass. In its own way, the experience haunted him. Within a month, he had packed everything he owned into the trunk of his car and decided to hit the road again, two weeks later arriving in Washington with no job, no friends, and $300 in his pocket.

In the next four years, Jody got married and began working as a financial analyst for a commercial bank. "It was the job I went to college for," he explained, "the job I was supposed to do." But something in him knew it wasn't what he was meant to do. He secretly wanted more. Fortunately, the long summer days allowed him to do what he really moved out west to do, which was explore the hidden treasures and dark trails of Deception Pass State Park.

He and his wife, Rebecca, built a house and began to settle into their life together—Jody as a banker and her as a teacher. But then one day, while helping them move into their new house, a friend said something that changed everything. She worked for Washington State Parks and mentioned that they were hiring park rangers. "Before the first box was moved into our new house," Jody said, "I had made up my mind. I was going to be a park ranger."

It may come as no surprise that a financial analyst does not have the credentials necessary to be a park ranger. So for the whole year after Jody made the decision to become a ranger, he worked at a bank during the day and went to school at night. This fact remained a secret at his day job until twelve months later when his dream came true. "I traded in my shirt and tie for the badge and flat hat," he recalled.

For a year, Jody worked in Spokane, driving home on the weekends to be with his wife. After a year of being apart, they finally sold their house and she joined him. At the same time as this transition, they learned they were going to be parents. Little did he know this little piece of news would one day affect his dream of being a park ranger.

How Was Your Day?

Last week, I was overseas. In a few days, I'll be in San Francisco. But for now, I'm home, making the most of being in Nashville, the city I moved to after touring as a musician for a year. My life, it seems, is full of variety. Every day I wake up to the sound of my two-year-old son talking over the baby monitor. Some days he wakes up crying, but today he's a chatterbox.

Pulling Aiden out of his crib, I carry him downstairs to make breakfast. Today we're having ham-and-cheese omelets. After breakfast, we play for an hour, and then his mom comes downstairs to take over. I make some coffee, take a shower, and head to work. It takes me two minutes to drive downtown, where my office is located. It's ten a.m. Opening my laptop, I check e-mail for an hour, then make a few calls with my cell phone.

Around noon, a friend and I meet for lunch. We chat about life, business, and fatherhood.

An hour goes by, and I return to the office to do some writing, squeezing in a half-chapter for a new book project and a quick blog post, which I schedule for later in the week. Feeling productive, I move on to more business-related matters. The rest of the afternoon is filled with preparation for an upcoming speaking gig and a smattering of text messages exchanged with my web developer, who's helping me build a piece of software.

This is a "normal" workday for me. Each is unique, filled with its own odd rhythms and appointments, and honestly, I kind of like it that way. But the hard part comes when someone asks me what my job is.

Instinctively, I say, "I'm a writer." But when I tell that person I don't spend most of my time writing books, they give me a funny look, and I have to further explain myself. If I say, "I'm a speaker," they'll expect me to say that I travel a lot or make most of my income through honorariums, but those things aren't true either.

I could, of course, tell them I run a website selling online products but that I'm not really an entrepreneur—not like my friends who run furniture stores and restaurants and such. They have staff members and a storefront. My business is just me. I write, speak, and look for ways to support my family. That's what I do.

The truth is I do all these things—they are all a part of me in their own way. And although each task might be hard to fit into a single job description, this is what I do. I learned there is a term for such a lifestyle, and it's not ADHD.

"It's called a portfolio life," my friend Keith told me.

"A what?" I said.

"A portfolio life. It means you aren't *just* a writer or a husband or a dad. You are all those things, and you need to embrace them."

"Oh," I said. "Cool."

Not long ago, I had lunch with an author friend. As we both scooped spoonfuls of gumbo into our mouths to warm ourselves against the winter air, I mustered the courage to ask a question.

"Hey, I've been meaning to ask you something, if you don't mind getting a little personal . . ."

He looked at me but said nothing. I continued.

"Um, so, uh, how do you make a living? Is it just through book advances and stuff? They can't be that much, can they?"

I knew for a fact he was writing a new book every few years, but the way his publisher stretched out the payments, he couldn't have been living off that money.

"Is it speaking?" I continued. I had explored this as a potential means of income and been disappointed.

My friend smiled politely. "Yeah, I make a little money from each of those." Then he grinned knowingly, looked around as if to see who was listening, and leaned forward to tell me something. "Well, to be honest," he whispered, "if all those things went away, I'd still be okay."

"What? Why?"

Smiling again, he said, "Because, and don't repeat this, but . . ." I was certain he was going to tell me he was a part of a drug cartel and invite me to get in on it. "Well, I do a little advising, some coaching, and mentoring for a few influential leaders."

"Oh," I said, trying to imagine who he was talking about. George W. Bush, maybe? Or George Clooney? I could only hope.

But the point, and what I walked away from that conversation with, was that my friend was living a portfolio life. Not only was he doing this out of financial necessity, he was also doing it because it's what he found most fulfilling. Most authors I know live portfolio lives. So do graphic designers and construction workers and self-employed people. What surprised me, though, is how many people I've met who found their callings through a portfolio of work. They didn't do just one thing but instead embraced a diverse set of activities that formed a complete identity. This is the way the world works now—and maybe the way it's supposed to work.

A Portfolio Perspective

By the year 2020, 40 to 50 percent of the American workforce will be freelancers. By 2030, it will be the majority.[2] Some of these people are being forced into self-employment caused by mass lay-offs due to the strain of a struggling economy, but others like myself have chosen such a path. Now, why on earth would we do that?

People are not robots, programmed to do one thing. We are multifaceted creatures with many varied interests. And though we may like to believe we were born to do just one thing, or perhaps we're comfortable with only having one career, the reality is most of us are hardwired for a handful of activities that when combined lead to our greatest satisfaction and best work.

The numbers are clear. A portfolio life is inevitable. The challenge, then, is not whether you should start building one, but *when*. We are complicated creatures, full of many interests and assorted passions. What do we do with all of them? We are not what we do for a living, but our life is made up of what we do. So how do we take this complexity into account? And what if our calling will never pay the bills? Do we give up the pursuit? Take a vow of poverty? Or is there another way?

The basic idea of a portfolio life is that instead of thinking of your work as a monolithic activity, what if you chose to see it as the complex group of interests, passions, and activities it is? And what if instead of identifying with a job description, you began to see the whole mass of things you do as *one* portfolio of activity?

This idea was first coined by Charles Handy in his book *The Age of Unreason*. In the book, Handy lays out five different types of work that make up your portfolio. They are: fee work, salary work, homework, study work, and gift work.

Fee and salary work are the only types of paid work and are somewhat self-explanatory: fee work means trading hours for dollars and a salary is a fixed income based on a job description. The unpaid work, however, is just as significant as the paid work; it's just different.

Homework is work that you do at home, like mowing the lawn or spending time with your family. Study work is any intentional education that contributes to any work you do in the future, like reading a book or taking a vocational class. And gift work is any volunteer experience you might do, including giving your time to a local homeless shelter or even taking someone out to lunch to give them helpful career advice.[3]

Handy then encourages what he calls "portfolio people" to organize their time not based on hours in a week, but rather days in a year. For example, if you need to make $50,000 per year and can figure out a way to make $250 a day, then you only need to work 200 days a year. The remaining 165 days can be spent on the rest of your portfolio. It's a useful way of organizing an unconventional career, which is likely what your calling will be for the first few years. But what if we applied this idea not just to work but to your whole life?

As I've already said, a calling is more than a career; it's the purpose and direction of your life. Which means that it doesn't just apply to what you do; it's who you are. So let's look at the four areas that make up the portfolio that is your life.

1. Work

At some point, you must come to grips with the fact that you will do many different things in life. Jobs will come and go, and careers won't last as long as you think they should. But in all those experiences, you will be growing. Every new experience contributes to the portfolio. Long gone are the days of graduating from high school or college, joining up with a company, and working there for forty years before retiring and collecting a pension.

In many cases, the organizations where we make our vocational homes won't be here five years from now. They will be acquired, go bankrupt, or morph into something different. That's just the way the world works now. Having a portfolio mindset toward work will make you a more well-rounded person and set you up for success in this new economy.

2. Home

Face it: not all of your life is work, and that's a good thing. We've spent much of this book exploring the concept that work is more important than many have made it. Your job is not mere drudgery; it is a calling, a noble vocation if you choose to see it that way. But at the same time, work is not all there is to the story of our lives. We are complex creatures, social animals, and how we invest our lives goes beyond where we punch a time clock. My own experience has taught me this many times over.

When I married Ashley, she vowed to be my biggest fan. I don't think either of us knew exactly what that meant at the time, but years later, after having published books and gone into business for myself, I can look back and see how she was a part of encouraging me through the process every step of the way. I couldn't have asked for a greater fan.

Having my wife by my side taught me that as important as dreaming is, an unshared dream is only a fantasy, an illusion. What makes the journey of vocation worthwhile is having someone to share your passion with. In my case, as a writer, without someone to support my work, the words I write start to become meaningless.

3. Play

I don't like the word *hobbies*. To me, those are things you never intend to take seriously. But we all have things we do for the pure love of the activity, regardless of whether they ever provide an income. Psychologists call this activity "play."

Recently researchers have come to realize how essential such activities are to our overall growth. Here's how Hara Marano, editor at large for *Psychology Today*, puts it: "We would all agree that play lifts stress from us. It refreshes us and recharges us. It restores our optimism. It changes our perspective, stimulating creativity . . .

But there is also evidence that play does much more. It may in fact be the highest expression of our humanity."[5]

Whatever you do to recharge at the end of the day isn't a diversion. Or at least, it doesn't have to be. It can be the very thing that keeps you healthy and sane. It can even serve to strengthen you as well as rest does. Your taste in music, the kinds of books you enjoy, even your favorite foods all contribute to the person you are and the portfolio you're creating—and therefore, make up your calling. Who knows how your past experiences and current interests might dance together to create something unique and wonderful? Play is how we keep our lives, and our work, interesting.

4. Purpose

There must be something bigger than what you do that guides you through the choices you make, the risks you take, and the opportunities you pursue. In many ways, this is the reason you work at all. It's the charity your company gives a percentage of profits to or the moral convictions guiding your values or the family that you're providing for. It's the work behind the work, and although it may not take eight hours a day, without a *why* behind the *what* that you do, your career becomes meaningless and ultimately useless.

Some, sadly, don't comprehend this until it's too late. On their deathbeds, they finally understand their purpose and how many opportunities they missed to make a difference. What a waste—to understand your purpose long after you can do anything about it. But for those who are willing to listen to the voice of calling and pay close attention to their lives, such a purpose may be known.

Charles Handy once said in an interview: "If you groan about your job or find it has become monotonous and boring, you need to ask yourself—what do you secretly want to do? Do it. You can have a breakpoint and reinvent yourself. Sensible people reinvent themselves every ten years."[6]

Choosing to see my calling as a portfolio, instead of as a single gig, has created more harmony and helped me make more sense of what I do than anything else. Maybe it will do the same for you too.

What Mastery Doesn't Mean

How do we take what we now know of portfolios and apply this knowledge to our own journeys of vocation? Once we have heard the call, answering is not enough. You have a responsibility to not only do what you were born to do, but to do it well.

For those who grew up on microwaves and prime-time TV, the concept of craft is lost to us. We did not grow up with an understanding of doing things with excellence; if it was expedient and got the job done, then it was good enough. In a world intent on following the path of least resistance, the goal is expediency, not excellence. Doing your work well is secondary to getting the job done. But what if doing things quickly and easily wasn't the point? What if our work was meant to not only serve the world but to make the *worker* better?

A writer was once asked by his well-meaning wife, "Why don't you write books people can read?" He wrote odd, almost poetic stories that few people understood. Dragging his family around

Europe while he tried to make a go at being an author, he was constantly plagued with financial difficulties. To make matters worse, his contemporaries criticized him for being nonsensical, even outrageous, and sometimes perverse. And now, his wife was joining the naysayers.

Such criticisms can wear on a person's soul, but he kept writing. In his mind, he knew what he was trying to do and that people would understand some day. For him, it wasn't about the money. It was about the craft, about honoring the work and doing what was his to do. The writer's name was James Joyce.

Joyce, who grew up in Ireland, fled his country after graduating college, at which point he rejected his Roman Catholic upbringing along with many other traditions and ties. He was determined to become a great writer with a brand-new style that would redefine our understanding of literature. And he did just that. In spite of his peers' misgivings, and even the jabs of a well-meaning wife, in 1999, fifty-eight years after his death, Joyce was voted by *Time* magazine as one of the most important people to have lived in the twentieth century.

When the world seems to conspire against you and when everyone around calls you a failure, true masters keep going. Even when others don't understand, masters recognize their allegiance is to a higher calling than pleasing the masses. Joyce was trying to do something the world had never seen. He was chasing a passion, and what we learn from such dedication is that what looks like irrelevance now can lead to legacy later. But passion alone is not enough to sustain the work. True mastery is about greatness, about doing something that pushes the limitations of what others think is possible or even sensible. Peter Senge, a professor at MIT, describes mastery as something that "goes beyond competence and skills . . . It means approaching one's life as a creative work."[7]

Mastery isn't about straight As or the highest salary in the company. It's not even about being the most popular in your field. It's about understanding your potential and then dedicating your life to pursuing that ideal. It means doing your absolute best. Why? Because the craft deserves it, because the calling requires it, and because maybe you'll be a better person for it. After all, this is the role of work in our lives—not only as a means to make a living, but as a tool to make us into who we were born to be.

We don't often think about how what we do affects who we are. Because a job is often just a job, it's easy to believe our activity doesn't affect our identity. It's true that you are not what you do, but you can become what you practice. And who are you practicing being at that job you hate, cutting corners to get the job done? It's time we reconnected with a more modern understanding of mastery.

—◊◊◊—

When I asked a successful musician how he went from making an average income for an artist to becoming an outlier in his industry, making a million dollars a year, his answer surprised me. Did he write a hit song or get some airplay on the radio? What was it that led to his skyrocketing success? "I stopped trying to be famous," he told me.

"What?" I said. "That's it?" I didn't understand. Weren't musicians supposed to be famous? Wasn't that the whole point of making a career out of your art? Didn't people have to know who you were? Apparently not. In fact, for my new friend, fame was more of a distraction than an ally.

"Yep," he answered. "I stopped trying to be famous and focused instead on trying to be successful."

I asked him what that word—*success*—meant to him and if he thought every musician should chase the money or become a millionaire.

"Of course not," he said. "Success isn't about money. It's about setting a goal—and then achieving it."

The Millionaire Musician had believed, as many do, that fame would one day lead to success, and he was disappointed. He thought he would eventually be able to take care of his family or not have to worry about touring two hundred days a year once he became famous, but that never happened. So he reset his expectations and focused on a different goal. Only then did he begin to see the results he had hoped for. For my friend, this meant more time with family, greater financial freedom, and a legacy for his children—those were his goals. The money that followed was a by-product.

What Is Work For?

Something strange happened to me on the road to my life's work. When I quit my job to become a full-time writer, with all the freedom in the world, I thought I had arrived, finally doing what I loved and getting paid for it. So why, after only a few months of self-employment, was I burnt out and ready to quit?

Work, for me, was always a necessary evil, something to do to take care of myself and pay the bills. Certainly work was good and worthwhile and I liked most of my jobs, but if I didn't need money, there would be no need to get a job. I was wrong. And this was the reason why after working for myself for only a few months, I was ready to throw in the towel. What I had ignored was the true meaning of work.

During that crisis, the question I had failed to ask myself, the one that we all need to ask at some point, was, "What is my work *for*?" Is it to make a living? That's the typical attitude and approach toward work, as a means to an end. We work to live, but we do not live to work. If the purpose of work is wealth and prosperity, what happens once you hit your goal of making enough money? Do you retire early? Some do. But even then, the goal seems small and somehow petty. If self-gratification is the ultimate reward, why are those with more often less happy? And why do people like Bill Gates and Bono take what they've accumulated and give it away? If it's not for fame or riches that we strive, then what are we working for?

During World War II, British writer Dorothy Sayers wrote a compelling essay called "Why Work?" and in it, she addressed the motivation for vocation. She posed a particular challenge that was appropriate for her context, asking what society would do with work after the war was over.

Many factories in Europe and the United States had been used to manufacture arms and supplies for the allied forces, but that was soon ending. During the war, production had gone through the roof; economies had thrived. And there was a clear and definite purpose for the work: to supply the allies with enough goods so that they could win the war. What would the factories and their workers do now, in a time of peace? How would people work when there was no central purpose to unite them? Sayers feared they would return to an inferior work ethic, which could create long-term problems for the West.

"The habit of thinking about work as something one does to make money is so ingrained in us," she wrote, "that we can scarcely imagine what a revolutionary change it would be to think about it instead in terms of the work done." If we could make this change and think of work the same way we think of play, treating it as something we do for pleasure, it could change the world.[8] In essence, Sayers was saying that the same attitude we have toward the pursuits we enjoy doing, we should have toward work, going on to say that work is not a means to an end. It is the end.

Every worker has a moral responsibility to ask deeper questions of the work. She wrote, "We should ask of an enterprise, not 'will it pay?' but 'is it good?'"[9] When you do what Sayers calls serving the work, you do what you were meant to do and you do it well. The rest is not up to you. Wealth may come. Fame too. But those are not the goal. Our job is to see work as a means of making us better, not just richer, people.

The work of psychology professor Mihaly Csikszentmihalyi demonstrates this. As a child, Csikszentmihalyi witnessed how the atrocities of World War II made it difficult for people to live meaningful lives after the war. They had been traumatized by the war and thus had little reason to feel happy. Was there a way for them to find meaning and even happiness in life again?

Increases in income—once you've reached a certain threshold above the poverty line—do not make people happier. "Increases in material well-being don't seem to affect how happy people are," Csikszentmihalyi said.[10]

So if fame and fortune aren't the secrets to happiness, what is? It's a mental state he calls "flow." Flow is the intersection of what you are good at and what challenges you—where difficulty and competency meet. When your competency exceeds the difficulty of a task, you are bored. And when the difficulty exceeds your competency, you are anxious. That was my problem: I was bored. So I did whatever I could think of to make my new job more difficult. And you know what? The boredom went away. Later, I realized the new challenges I had stepped into gave me a sense of purpose that was lacking.

This was the same issue facing the workers in Europe and the United States after the war. How would they avoid a sense of purposelessness? They needed to find their flow, understanding that the challenge wasn't in producing something for some far-off cause. It was in the work itself.

Here's how Csikszentmihalyi described that feeling you get when you are in a state of flow: "You know that what you need to do is possible to do, even though difficult, and sense of time disappears. You forget yourself. You feel part of something larger."[11] If the work we do is only about our own personal success or recognition, then we will eventually lose interest or become overwhelmed with anxiety. But if it's about a greater good, if we are here to serve the work and not the other way around, then we get up every day with a new challenge, a purpose. Which sounds a lot like a calling.

We are caretakers of our vocations, stewards entrusted with a vision that is bigger than us. Our responsibility is not to hoard our gifts but to use them in challenging ways so that others can benefit. In short, your calling is a gift, one that is intended to be given away. Calling is a conduit for life, allowing us to bring our skills and passions together in a satisfying, meaningful way.

The Road to Mastery

After receiving a promotion that forced him and his family to relocate, Jody Maberry moved away from Spokane to work several more years at a different park out west.[12] He thought his dream was to be a ranger, but when he saw the personal cost, he wasn't so sure anymore. He wasn't spending much time with his family, and his kids were growing up fast. To make matters worse, the park system was in trouble, and he wasn't sure how secure his job was.

After an internal struggle, Jody decided to leave his job at the park to focus on his family. Returning to school again, he got an MBA and went to work for a small construction company helping them with the administrative side of the business. He also relocated his family into town, something they had never done before. For the first time, his kids had neighbors—and they loved it. To this day, he doesn't regret it.

But even now, years later, there is a hunger still inside Jody that will not go away. A year after leaving his position at the park, he started to feel the itch again. At school, he would be reminded of ways that he could apply what he was learning to his previous job as a ranger. In conversations with friends, he would find himself missing the work. "Parks began tugging at me again," he recalled. "This time, I knew not to let it call for too long."

Today Jody works as a consultant with businesses on their strategic planning and marketing. He's considering getting back into working with parks again someday, but for now he feels like he made the right choice.

When I video-chatted with Jody, I asked him if he had any regrets. "No, I don't," he said. "Sometimes I miss it, but I don't have any regrets." He told me about men he knew—former park rangers—who had to make tough choices like he did. They had to move their families or get laid off. "Being a ranger was everything to them; they loved the job," he said. But many had to grieve the loss of their dream when they chose their families over parks.

Some went on to be fish and wildlife officers, others state troopers, and even others school teachers. But their dream of being a park ranger was gone, as it was for Jody, and they had to move on. "It's really sad," he said. "In many ways, you are a park ranger first and a dad or husband second." It's part of the job, he admits, but something about it always unnerved him.

Maybe moving on is part of the process. Maybe a calling is always evolving, never allowing you to stand still in one place for too long. Now Jody is using both his business background and his park experience to help build the next generation of park leaders. When we spoke, he had recently launched a podcast called The Park Leaders Show, which features guest interviews with other rangers and experts and is quickly becoming an industry resource. A lot of the job of being a park ranger involves management and business skills that you have to learn on your own. "There's no training for that," he told me. The podcast provides such training.

On the show, Jody was able to interview Jack Hartt, his first manager, who helped him get started as a ranger. At one point in the conversation, Jody said something to indicate that he missed being a ranger. Jack replied, "You may miss being a park ranger, but if you can make this [podcast] work, you will impact more people than you ever could working in a park."

Looking back, Jody can see how everything in his life, even the unexpected turns and disappointments, helped him get to where he is now. He couldn't be doing what he's now doing without the many weird twists in his story that forced him to pivot at opportune times. "I couldn't have done this," he said, "without being a park ranger for eight years. And I couldn't have done it without being in business and having a nontraditional park ranger story." To him, it's all connected.

So how does Jody see his calling now? Has it changed or evolved? "I was called to parks, not to be a park ranger," he said, explaining that he better understands now what he was meant to do. "And even when I tried to leave, I was drawn back." In his experience, this is how a calling works. It's something that will not leave you alone, a beckoning toward the work for which you were made. And for Jody, it came and went at different seasons, growing and changing as he did.

"Don't search for your calling," he said. "Explore, try new things, keep your feet moving. Something will grab you. It will call to you. It is no different than falling in love. You can't sit on your couch and decide you are going to marry a certain girl. You fall in love after sharing experiences, joy, challenges, maybe even heartbreak. All of which could not have happened without leaving your couch, being involved, and meeting the one girl you can't stop thinking about."

At different times, Jody had to walk away from what he thought was his calling. He loved his job, but he had responsibilities to his family that trumped his job. For him, a calling is not just a position; it's a life lived well. And perhaps the same is true for you and me.

When I met Jody during a trip to Washington State, he took me around his old stomping grounds, driving me to the top of Mount Spokane and pointing out the sights, telling me stories along the way. As he did, I could tell that although he left his job as a ranger years ago, the job never fully left him. "A calling does not mean a specific job," he said. "I am no longer a park ranger, but it does not mean I have to walk away from my calling. I can instead apply my strengths to add value to the cause in another way."[13]

PART THREE

Completion

SEVEN

Your Magnum Opus

What Legacy Looks Like

A life isn't significant except for
its impact on other lives.

—JACKIE ROBINSON

Your calling is not a job. It is your entire life.

I'm not sure what I was expecting visiting my first mud hut in the middle of Africa, but this was not it. I was not expecting hope. "Is this where you live?" our guide asked the little girl as we marched up the dirt path to her home. Otherwise stoic, her attitude brightened as we reached the top of the hill and were greeted by her parents—at least, we thought they were her parents.

Sam, the man of the house, was quick to correct this misunderstanding. Nine-year-old Kevin was his sister-in-law. He and his wife, Christine, took her in after her mother disappeared. The mother suffered from some form of mental illness and had the unfortunate habit of abandoning her children. So they decided to raise Kevin as their own. And when you ask them about this or praise their kindness, they get embarrassed.

Three sturdy mud huts with thatched roofs made up the family's home: one was a kitchen, and the other two were bedrooms. As we toured the premises, I noticed each building was well kept, the floors neatly swept and things put away where they belonged. There was a familiar order to the place, a pattern that felt like home. They were modest people, but you could tell they took great pride in what they had, especially Christine.

Life was tough for them, no question about it. In the past year, the couple had lost twin baby boys, a wound they were still healing from. Their son, Augustine, was deaf, and they didn't have access to opportunities like specialized schooling that would certainly make life easier.

Sam was born to a poor farming family in Lira, Uganda, which is located in the northern part of the country where a civil war ravaged the land for two decades. Despite his parents' limited means, they gave him a plot of land on which he began farming and raising his family. "It's rare to see a man stay after the kids come," one of the trip leaders told me. Men in that culture tend to leave once children come into the picture, but Sam was not that kind of man.

After we visited with the family for a while, Sam showed me a small shop on the side of a nearby road, where he sold small items like bags of cooking oil and matches.

I promptly peppered him with questions: "How much do you make off of each item? What's your profit margin? When can you order new inventory?"

He knew all the answers.

I even asked if he had a goal of how much money he wanted to make. This, I've learned, is a question most people don't know the answer to, and one that leads to true success. You have to have a goal, to know where you're going, in order to get there. It seems obvious, but so many people chase after a dream without any idea of what they're really trying to achieve. But Sam was different.

"Five million," he said without hesitation.

That's how much money he needed to make to send his son to a special needs school and build a house that wasn't made of mud. Without trying to seem too conspicuous, I pulled out my phone and opened the calculator app, doing a quick currency conversion. It equaled $2,000.

"I think you will meet your goal, Sam." I said, smiling.

His family had to walk two miles every day to get clean drinking water. They didn't have electricity or any modern conveniences. They cooked all their meals over a fire and lived off of less than a few dollars a day. Yet all around his home were plants like sorghum and mango trees, life-giving fruits and vegetables and grains that ensured his family would not go hungry.

Sam was doing more than subsisting. He was working hard to not only make ends meet but to improve his life and create a future for his children. When we said goodbye to the man with the infectious smile, I realized how wealthy he was.

Poverty and wealth are concepts that cannot be defined merely by what you have or make. Is the lawyer who makes $450,000 a year and spends half a million rich? Are his habits sustainable? What about the mom I met a couple of years ago in the slums of Guatemala, who sweeps her house clean every morning before going to work in the market so she can send her kids to school—is she poor? I don't say this to make light of those who live on next to nothing, nor do I want to minimize the luxury from which I am able to write this. But what I have learned, not from the suburbs but from the slums, is that poverty is more than a context. It's a mindset. I have met rich people in some of the poorest parts of the planet and I have met bankrupt people living in million-dollar homes.

Sam isn't going to be poor, if we can even call him that, for long. He has the opportunity, the means, and the will to change his life. His demeanor was different from the vibe I got entering the slums of Kampala. That was a different kind of poverty; there was little hope there. But in Sam's eyes, I saw something I wanted, something powerful and infectious. His dream was not for him; it was for his family. And that gave me hope. If Sam can find meaning and motivation in rural Uganda with nothing more than a hoe to farm and a shack to start a business, then what's stopping you and me with all the tools at our disposal? How do we take a calling, however extraordinary or ordinary it may seem, and do as Sam has done? How do we turn our work into something generous?

Our circumstances rarely dictate what we can do with our lives, and that man who was making a life for himself and his loved ones in the African bush taught me more than any millionaire ever could. For him, the work is both the means and the end to a better life. He's doing what he loves and doing it for the people he loves.

Success Isn't About You

I always thought pursuing a dream was about you, that it was inherently selfish. But I couldn't have been more wrong. It wasn't until I got everything I wanted in life that I realized none of it was for me.

"I think it's time that I move on," I told my boss of seven years, who had mentored me for much of that time. He immediately sat up in his chair, looking at me, not saying a word. "I, uh . . . well, I think it's time. The money's there. The family support is there. My passion is there. The only thing that would keep me from doing this is, well, I wouldn't want to disappoint you."

For a moment, he just stared at me without saying anything. Then finally he spoke up: "Jeff, I'm not disappointed in you. I'm *proud* of you. In fact, I've been waiting for this conversation. I've seen this coming for a while. It's about time you went off and did something on your own."

A few months later, I began working for myself. That's when the really hard work began. Before leaving my job, I had saved up enough money to live on for at least six months, if not a year (but that would have been really stretching it). The idea was to not have to worry about income for a while so that I wouldn't be stressed the first month on the job. I always wanted to be able to take my time building a business. But there was just one problem with having all that savings: I wasn't motivated to work.

After seeing work as a means of making a paycheck for so many years, I didn't have a good reason to go to work when money was no longer an issue. For a couple of months, I really struggled with motivation, with knowing why I should be working. This lack of motivation turned into laziness, which devolved into depression. If I didn't need to work, what did I need to do, and why?

Eventually, I did go back to work, but with different intentions. During my two-month funk, I called my friend Stu, who owns a successful software company, to ask how he dealt with motivation. "Jeff," he said, "I live in a small town, and my standard of living hasn't really changed since I started working for myself." At a time when he was starting to make more money than he would ever need, Stu went on a trip to Africa and his eyes were opened to a whole new world of possibility. In Kenya, he saw how much of a difference opportunity and a good education could make in a person's life. He realized that instead of feeling guilty, he could use the gifts he was born with, some of which he didn't earn or deserve, to help other people. "After that, I realized I was good at making money and didn't need to feel bad about that. I could do what I do best and use it for good. When I returned home, I started working not for myself but for all those people I met in Africa."

A few years later, I had a similar experience, having raised enough money through my blog to help build an income-generating workshop for women living in a leper camp just outside of Mombasa, Kenya. Work, it seems, was never meant to be something we do just to make a living. It was meant to be a means of making a difference—in our own lives and in the lives of others. The problem today is that many of us see our jobs just as a duty, something we're obligated to do to pay the bills. Or we see it as a means of improving our lives, of making so much money we can buy all the things we've ever wanted. But neither option will satisfy.

This me-first way of looking at vocation doesn't work. When you look around at the world, you see a curious trend in the lives of some billionaires and movie stars. They aren't content to simply savor the fruit of their labor, but neither do they let their largesse lead to unproductive guilt. They understand that feeling guilty, in and of itself, doesn't accomplish anything. Instead, they're using their resources and influence to improve other people's lives.

Leveraging their connections and celebrity, understanding that people will listen to them, they're trying to do something good.

A few generations ago, men went to work or war and rarely got to see life beyond their careers. A generation ago, our parents had to answer the question of what they would do with the last third of their lives. How would they spend their retirement? Would it be squandered on silly things or invested in significance?

But now, the question of legacy isn't a matter of *if* you live long enough or *when* you retire; it's a matter of what you will do with what you have right now. You don't have to earn a living for thirty years to turn around and spend the next thirty giving it away. If significance is what matters to you, you can structure your life and work in a way that allows you to live your legacy now. In fact, your giving doesn't have to be a by-product of your success; it can be the very thing that drives it in the first place.

"We Are Your Symphony"

In the film *Mr. Holland's Opus*, Glenn Holland is a frustrated music teacher trying to compose a masterwork in the margins of life. He never succeeds—at least not in the way he hopes. Every time he gets close to completing his symphony, some new complication arrives, and his work must be put on hold.

A touring musician on sabbatical, Mr. Holland takes the open music instructor position at a high school because he thinks it will give him more time to compose. But as the demands of the job increase and the pressures from home build, he realizes how wrong he was. Over the course of his teaching career, which he thought would only be a temporary commitment to pay some bills, he inspires students to continue playing music, struggles to be a good dad and faithful husband, and battles a stubborn school board that ultimately has him fired, all while slowly picking away at his composition.

When Glenn learns his son is deaf, he realizes Cole will never be able to appreciate music the same way he does. In one scene, the two get in a fight when the father tells his son that he is sad because John Lennon was just shot and that Cole wouldn't understand. Most of Mr. Holland's life is full of moments like this—scenes of frustration where he feels misunderstood or simply overlooked, as if he's the only one with dreams bigger than his life can contain.

By the end of the movie, Mr. Holland is a cynical old man, tired of school board bureaucracy and resigned to the fact that in spite of his dreams, he will never be a master composer. After his last day of school, his family is escorting him to the exit when he hears music coming from the gymnasium. Curious, he opens the doors to an auditorium full of hundreds of students, teachers, and alumni, all gathered to wish him well and celebrate the impact he had on their lives. In the crowd, he sees many familiar faces, including one apathetic student who used to challenge his authority.

Another former student, Gertrude Lang, who is now the state governor, acts as emcee and welcomes everyone, explaining how Mr. Holland had an impact on her life, as he has done for everyone in the auditorium. Then she remarks on how Holland feels like he has misspent a great part of his life. "Rumor had it," she says, "he was always working on this symphony of his, and this was going to make him famous, rich. Probably both. But Mr. Holland isn't rich, and he isn't famous. At least not outside of our little town." Then she looks at the man who was her favorite teacher and says, "Mr. Holland, *we* are your symphony."[1]

Gertrude then asks him to come onstage as the curtains pull back to reveal a full orchestra band, ready to play "An American Symphony" by Glenn Holland. With tears in his eyes, he conducts the symphony he spent three decades of his life composing, an effort he thought had been lost forever.[2] It's a moment of clarity for both the audience and the protagonist, a man who felt he had missed his calling, that he had wasted his life on a pursuit less significant. And he was wrong.

Sometimes all the little things in life aren't interruptions to our calling. They are the most important part. "Life is what happens to you while you're busy making other plans," John Lennon wrote in a song to his son, Sean.[3] We see this come true in Mr. Holland's life, as he can now see the full picture of his calling, understanding that every frustration had a purpose and that when he felt farthest from his true reason for living, he was actually much closer than he realized.

Life has a funny way of teaching us that sometimes the most important stuff is the ordinary stuff. The smallest moments, the ones we think are insignificant, are the ones we will cherish the most. As you endeavor to do something amazing with your life, don't forget that without people to support your dream, your work will always be incomplete. A life filled with achievements and accolades but lacking those people necessary to celebrate those moments is not much of a life at all.

In your pursuit of a worthwhile vocation, you will be tempted to rush past these times. These are the moments you get interrupted by a colleague at the water cooler or when your toddler tugs on your pant leg when you have just one more e-mail to send. These are the times when you get distracted, when the whole world seems to be plotting against your productivity. But there is often a purpose in these moments—to remind you that a calling is more than a career; it is a life lived well. And the very things you try to avoid are what you need the most to make this story matter.

I used to think that your calling was about doing something good in this world. Now I understand it's about becoming someone good—and letting that goodness impact the world around you. Which means that you won't fully appreciate the whole story you're living until the end. But for now, if you are intentional and willing to appreciate the fact that you don't see the whole narrative, you can enjoy more of the journey.

Now I Become Myself

"What kind of writer do you want to be?" my friend Marion asked me. I didn't know what to say. Should I say Salinger or Shakespeare, maybe pick someone a little more contemporary, a little more successful? What was the right answer? I was unsure.

The truth was I wanted to be like a lot of different writers, but what I really wanted was what they had. Fame, talent, money. But those are lousy things to wish for when someone asks you what kind of writer you want to be, so I had to think of something more thoughtful to say. Even if you want those things, you certainly can't say so out loud.

We all have too many choices in this world. Freedom is a great thing, but freedom without restriction can be paralyzing. When it comes to vocation, we need some boundaries as well, parameters that allow us to focus. The good news is that the path to your life's work is already laid out for you. It has been there since the beginning of your life, and it's quite different from that of your friends or those famous people you admire.

When we talk about finding a calling, we're not just seeking an activity. We're looking for an identity, an understanding of who we are. We want to be complete, to make sense of the story of our lives. But whether we recognize it or not, this quest we've been talking about is not just a physical one; it's a spiritual one. It is, in a way, a journey of becoming.

"Now I become myself," May Sarton wrote. "It's taken / Time, many years and places; / I have been dissolved and shaken, / Worn other people's faces."[4] We all do this on occasion. We spend too much time pretending to be someone else. We try to recreate a life we admire instead of the one we were born for. We vainly expend energy and effort on pursuits that are bound for failure—all because we're afraid of being our true selves. But the lucky ones discover a different path. Or rather, they forge one where there was no way, departing from expectation in order to become who they are.

To be called is not enough. You must become your calling, a choice that happens only if you make it. Why do so few people do this? What's really at stake here? As with any journey, there is ris danger, the likelihood of failure. And most would rather play than be rejected by their friends or fall on their faces for the world to see. So they live lives of safety and relative obscurity, focusing on the things they enjoy and are praised for instead of daring to do something great. And time creeps by, taunting those who did not live.

Ezra Pound aptly wrote of such people: "And the days are not full enough / And the nights are not full enough / And life slips by like a field mouse / Not shaking the grass."[5] That feeling you feel when you see a great movie or read a powerful story—you know that itch? It's telling you there is more life in you yet to be lived. Ancient myths and legends speak to this. Every hero's journey included some sacred task that culminated in a deeper understanding of who they were born to be. And how was this done? Through a personal quest—some great feat that required every talent, skill, and strength they could muster. In other words, they had to work.

Every day you and I face a choice: to either pursue our authentic selves or a shadow of the real thing. We either do what is expected of us, or we listen to that voice of intuition deep inside promising something more significant. And as we pick up our hammers and scalpels, as we sit down in front of our laptops or climb onboard the bus for another tour, as we endeavor to do meaningful work in the world, we are becoming ourselves. We are, as Viktor Frankl wrote, looking for a reason to be happy. Fulfillment isn't just for the elite few who find a purpose for life; it's for everyone. And that potential exists in each and every one of us. You have everything you need to be your whole self; it's already in you. Now you just have to become it.

A calling isn't something new and shiny. Often it's something old and predictable, a familiar face that's easily taken for granted, an old habit or hobby that comes back into our lives. It's our true self, shared with the world. But sometimes it takes a wake-up call for us to see that this work that we're doing is more significant than we realize.

Classroom teacher Gloria Stronks learned this lesson one day when she took some time off. "I've hired a substitute for the next two days," the principal told her. "I want you to visit the homes of each of your children. You need stay only ten minutes in each home." Then she added, "You won't find fathers at home because many of them are in prison. I just want you to understand your students."

Gloria never intended to be a teacher of small children. Her husband was a graduate student, and she needed a job, so she took the only position available as the head of a class of forty-seven third graders. Her visit to the children's homes was nothing short of incredible. The homes were shacks with dirt floors. The children slept on those floors or in some car seat from the junkyard. Here is her recollection:

> The mothers spoke poorly and seemed frightened to have me visit. I returned to school, amazed that my students could learn as well as they did and recognizing the fine teaching that had occurred earlier so that now each one of these children could read at least at a mid-second grade level. Those teachers had been the most important adults in the lives of the children . . . and now I was one of them.[6]

Gloria's feeling of ingratitude was replaced with a deep sense of honor. She went from resenting her job to embracing it. Sometimes, a ca...ng is simply accepting your role in a story that is bigger than you. So when my friend asked what kind of writer I wanted to be, I said the most natural thing that came to mind: "I want to be the kind of writer I'm supposed to be."

Missing the Call

The easiest way to miss your calling is to ignore the call. Maybe it feels too risky, or maybe you feel too old and silly chasing a dream that now seems out of reach. We keep putting off starting for "someday," which never comes. This is common, and we tend to excuse our lack of action, even rationalizing it to each other.

Most people find themselves in careers that do anything but inspire them, and this can lead to complacency. *Why would I take such a risk? My friends and family members aren't. Doing so would make me weird, maybe even alienate me from those who love me.* So they don't ever find the time, and sadly they "die with their song still in them," as Oliver Wendell Holmes once wrote.[7]

Another way to miss your calling is to treat it as an event instead of a lifestyle. Remember: your vocation is more of a magnum opus than a single masterpiece. It's an entire body of work, not a single piece. You will spend your life creating it, and if you stop too soon or don't see your entire life as a means of accomplishing that task, you could miss it.

Recently over lunch while we were discussing the topic of calling and purpose, a friend said, "Maybe my purpose in life was to simply raise my daughters, and *they're* going to go do something great. Maybe that's all I was meant to do, and my purpose is now fulfilled. And everything else is just gravy. I would be okay with that."

He's onto something in that he sees his purpose as something that is bigger than him, a task he was born to accomplish that will send ripples into eternity. But your calling is not a single event in your life; it's the whole body of work you make—including your job, your relationships, and the legacy you leave behind. If you see it as something other than that, you may stop short of the goal. You can, in fact, not live up to your potential. Maybe you answered the call but at some point gave up. You started down the road but decided to retire or settle, and at some point, you let go. You settled for good when you were called to greatness.

In the movie *Finding Forrester*, Sean Connery plays a writer in his latter years of life, a recluse, confined to his home, who doesn't care much for visitors. This doesn't bode well for the young college student who tracks him down in search of a mentor. At first, Forrester dismisses the young man—in fact, he cusses him out and chases him away. But eventually, the two become friends, and the young man finds his way in life largely due to the mentorship. At the very end of the story, the old man realizes that although he wrote a best-selling novel years ago, his purpose wasn't over once he achieved a surprising amount of fame.[8]

The same is true for us and the way we pursue our callings. Success isn't the goal; legacy is. Ultimately, we are called to call others; we are given gifts to be given away. All that to say: when you find yourself at the pinnacle of personal greatness, y just be getting started.

The Lesson of Stephen King's Desk

Stephen King wrote in his memoir that for years he approached his craft wasted, treating his vocation as competition with the rest of life. At the pinnacle of his success, and in the depths of his addiction, he bought a desk. A possession he had always dreamed of, the desk was "the sort of massive oak slab that would dominate a room"[9]—he placed it in the middle of his study where he tirelessly went to work every day.

After getting sober with the intervention of his family, King got rid of the huge desk and replaced it with a smaller one, which he put in the corner of his office instead of in the center of the room. His children would regularly come up to the office, which was now more a living room than a retreat center, to watch sports games and movies and to eat pizza. He never complained. What he learned from this tale of two desks and his struggle with an addiction that nearly cost him his family was that "life isn't a support system for art. It's the other way around."[10]

This was what Sam in Uganda reminded me of and what Jody Maberry did so well for his family. Life is not an inconvenience to the work we dream of; it's the reason we do it in the first place. A calling does not compete with or even complement your life. Your life, when lived well, becomes your calling—your magnum opus. And just like Mr. Holland, we won't appreciate this until the end.

Several years ago, I wrote a list of dreams and goals with dates assigned to each. On that list at the ten-year mark was the goal, "Write and publish a book." A year later, the goal was realized. After a year of late nights and early mornings, of fighting with my wife about when I would come to bed and often breaking that promise, of countless misunderstandings with colleagues and arguments over where my allegiances lay, and three hundred days of doubting myself, I had finally done it. I'd written a book. And I was proud.

When the big day arrived, nothing went right. Visiting the local Barnes & Noble, I failed to find a single copy of my book on the shelves. Within a few hours, Amazon ran out of its short supply, and people I had told to go buy the book were telling me they couldn't find it anywhere. Embarrassed and feeling sorry for myself, I left the house to run some errands and to get a drink with a friend. We were supposed to be celebrating, but instead I wanted to commiserate.

A few hours later, he dropped me off at my house. Crossing the threshold, I stepped into a house full of people who shouted, "Surprise!" My wife had thrown me a party with twenty of my closest friends. After walking around, greeting and thanking everyone, I reached for a cupcake and saw on our dining room table a small white envelope with a card inside. The card, which was from my wife, said, "It was never a question of *if*. It was always a matter of *when*." She who had pledged to be my biggest fan had been rooting for me from the very beginning.

As you strive to achieve your life's work, be careful of at what costs you chase it. It will be easy to resent those closest to you, to

make your biggest supporters into your worst enemies. To hoard
your work away from the rest of life. You may be tempted to see
every relationship not as a lifeline, but as a competing force, something to be mistrusted. And in doing this, you may destroy the
very things that could save you.

Consumed by the Calling

I often wonder about my grandfather, who was a journalist, artist,
and alcoholic for much of his life. A talented pianist and play-
wright, Grandpa was a man I admired—a deep thinker, a complex
character full of frustration and sometimes unexplained sadness.
There is much about that man that is still a mystery. But one thing
I do know is that surrounded by the books he loved, with eyes
full of regret, he died at the hands of his addiction. Jaundiced and
glassy-eyed, staring at me with a softness I will never forget, he
gripped my hand and smiled. A few days later, his major organs
completely shut down, and he was gone.

I have no doubt that my grandfather was called to be an artist.
But I also know that for a season of life he let his calling consume
him. So whenever I snap at my wife or lose patience with my son,
I try to remember this and that Stephen King quote. Life is not a
support system for your work; your work is a support system for
your life. No amount of success is worth losing the ones you love
the most. I am still learning this, still swallowing my pride and
ambition and learning to move my desk out from the middle of the
room. Each time I take the day off to go to the zoo with my family,

I don't regret it. Every time I close the laptop to watch a movie with my wife or get up with my son in the middle of the night before a speaking gig, I remember these are not interruptions to the call; they are the most significant parts of the process.

There is an old episode of *The Simpsons* in which Homer leaves his despised job at the nuclear power plant to pursue his dream of working at a bowling alley. When he hears news around town that his wife is pregnant and that he won't be able to support his family, he is forced to return to the power plant, where his former boss, Mr. Burns, makes him beg for his job back. To further humiliate him, Mr. Burns places a plaque in Homer's office that says, "Don't forget; you're here forever." But by the end of the episode, Homer has taken all the pictures of his daughter Maggie and taped them to the plaque so that it now reads, "Do it for her."[11]

In the journey toward our callings, there will be roadblocks and inconveniences, setbacks and slowdowns that we may mistake for distractions when in fact they are as much a part of the calling as the job itself. Right now, a good friend is in the middle of realizing this as he transitions from a career as a teacher to a new job as a financial advisor. At first, he resented the fact that he was going to have to leave his job, which he loved, so that his wife could stay home to raise their kids. It felt like selling out and giving up a dream for something that paid the bills. But as he spent the greater part of a year wrestling over the decision, he realized that any good dream is one worth sharing, and sometimes worth sacrificing, for others. This doesn't mean we need to give up on our deepest longings, but it does mean that a calling is about more than *me*.

When I was in Africa, I asked the Ugandan farmer Sam what

he and his family did for fun. Looking around at his surroundings, I noticed there wasn't much and knew that summers were hot there. What did they do all day long when they weren't farming or fetching water? As soon as I asked the question, Sam frowned. Then he shook his head. The translator repeated the question. He shook his head again, confused.

"You know," I repeated. "Fun. Like, what do you do when you're not working?"

He nodded as the translation came through, then thought for a moment and finally spoke.

"We do everything together—and to us, it is fun."

Conclusion

The Work Is Never Done

Art is never finished, only abandoned.

—LEONARDO DA VINCI

Your calling is not a destination. It is a journey that doesn't end until you die.

In a former life, Ed Cathey was a physical therapist, but I never knew that man. The man I knew was no doctor; there was nothing clinical about him. At the ripe age of seventy-something, Ed, who had long since left his practice at Vanderbilt Hospital, held down a part-time job as a chaplain at the Nashville Rescue Mission. He had tried to retire but instead ended up attending to the spiritual, emotional, and physical needs of homeless men who congregated in the overcrowded courtyard every day.

To be honest, Ed looked out of place. A clean-cut African American gentleman from Chicago, who spoke the most proper English I'd ever heard, didn't quite blend in with the roughneck crowd of drug addicts, disabled veterans, and thugs you encountered on a daily basis at the mission. Always wearing neatly pressed button-down shirts tucked tidily into well-ironed slacks, he was the picture of elegance and grace. Which contrasted with the drunken shouts and raucous hollering often echoing through the concrete walls of the mission.

What was Ed doing there?

Sometimes men would approach him and try to give him a high-five or some kind of handshake. Ed would have none of that; he always returned such gestures with an awkward smile and polite nod, followed by a pat on the shoulder. I never knew why he did this but suspected it was because he couldn't relate and maybe because he wanted more for those men than their loud greetings and macho handshakes.

"Thanks, son," he would say, often squeezing their arms and then moving on.

Sometimes they would retort sarcastically, "I'm not your son!" But often, I would see the men's gazes soften as they stared into Ed's warm eyes. I wondered if anyone had ever called them that before. Later he told me that for some, he was the only father they ever knew.

Ed ended up at the mission, and had been working there for nearly fifteen years, not because he had a passion for the poor or because he had any particular burden for the homeless. In fact, he told me this was the last place he ever thought he'd end up. But he had a friend on the board who invited him to visit the mission one day. After touring the facilities, Ed was asked if he would consider becoming a chaplain at the mission. After some hesitation, he relented, agreeing to work there a few days a week, counseling and praying with men who were struggling to escape their situations.

Ed had worked hard to build a life for himself, a fact in which he seemed to have just the right amount of pride. He had disciplined himself to rise above what was expected of him at a time when black men weren't given many options to succeed. And here he was, back with the kind of people he had tried not to be like his whole life. It was humbling, I'm sure. To be honest, I probably judged Ed a little. Did he really have compassion for these men, or did he merely tolerate them? There were times when it seemed he was quite uncomfortable around them. So why did he keep spending his time, which was becoming a more valuable commodity with age, at the mission? Why here? What did he have to gain from spending his remaining years of life with such men? I once heard a story from one of the other chaplains, which answered the question.

One day outside the mission doors, lying on the ground in the courtyard, was a small, emaciated man who appeared to be either dead or comatose. Like many, he had passed out from some form of intoxication or drug-induced slumber. Frail and fraught with disease, likely infected with HIV, he was covered in his own urine and feces. Sadly, it was not uncommon to see a man like this, passed out due to drinking or drugs, who would then wake up to a mess of his own making. When this man awoke, he was too weak to move. Some passed him by, laughing and even playing jokes on him, while others ignored him.

But when Ed—clean, proper, doctoral Ed—saw this man and realized he couldn't get up on his own, he went to him. And crouching in his khakis, he placed his arms underneath the man's head and legs, careful not to hurt him, and lifted him up, pulling the damp, dirty man close to his chest and carrying him inside where he could receive proper care. After hearing that story, I never again questioned why Ed was at the mission. I knew. He was there because he was called.

Hemingway's Regret and Niggle's Redemption

In 1961, the writer A. E. Hotchner went to see his good friend Ernest Hemingway in an honest attempt to save his life. Hotchner was an editor, novelist, and one of Hemingway's biographers. After hearing Hemingway repeatedly complain about everything from taxes to his clothes, Hotch asked a simple question of his friend: "Papa, why do you want to kill yourself?"

The author responded, "What do you think happens to a man going on sixty-two when he realizes that he can never write the books and stories he promised himself? Or do any of the other things he promised himself in the good days?"

Hotch encouraged Hemingway that he still had great work in him and that he had written a beautiful book about Paris (which would later become *A Moveable Feast*), but Hemingway would hear none of it, saying the best parts of those stories had been written long ago. "And now," he said, "I can't finish it."

"But perhaps it is finished, and it is just reluctance . . ."

"Hotch, if I can't exist on my own terms, then existence is impossible. Do you understand? That is how I've lived, and that is how I *must* live—or not live."

That was the last time Hotch saw his friend. Later that year, Hemingway lost his life to a self-inflicted gunshot wound.[1] Beloved by the world, Papa died a lonely, depressed man. In the end, what he had accomplished—publishing several best-selling books, traveling all over the world, winning the Nobel Prize for literature—was just not enough.

Every person faces the ultimate insufficiency of their work. Every worker knows the limits of their labor. And every person who is called understands that there is danger in such a compulsion; the work can consume you if you let it. There is something in a compulsion that makes a person creative—it is the will to not quit, to obsess over a single phrase or paint blotch until it is just right. That thing that makes you stay up late or get up early or spend an inordinate amount of time on that project that no one will see—that's what makes the work great. But there is also an implicit warning in such compulsions.

There is a great temptation in the pursuit of meaningful work to lose yourself in the process. That's what an addiction promises: total annihilation of self. You begin to no longer be able to dissociate yourself from what you've created. And this is dangerous territory. The real job in the work we do is to understand this temptation and use it to our advantage. Every compulsion is not a calling, but your life's work may begin with a prompting so strong it borders on obsession. What you must do is learn to temper it, to live in the tension of being driven without driving yourself mad. To master the craft so it doesn't master you. This is the only way to master the art of work, to recognize the inclinations in us that, when left unchecked, would destroy us.

What good, then, is it to pursue a calling if the pursuit may destroy you? How do we balance this tension between the ceaseless call of work and life itself? We must recognize what we don't know. Many world-famous artists were considered fools by their contemporaries. Fortunately, their work endured, maybe sometimes in spite of themselves. But their lives offer an important lesson: we don't have to give in to despair. We can trust that legacy follows faithfulness. There is always a deeper story.

—◈—

During the Second World War, British author J. R. R. Tolkien, who would go on to write one of the greatest fantasy novels of the twentieth century, was contemplating death. Would he live through such turbulent times or die in the middle of completing his life's work? He didn't know, and the possibility of not completing such a task haunted him. To process his fears, Tolkien wrote a short story about a man named Niggle.

Niggle was an artist who was always getting distracted from his work. Neighbors and friends would ask favors of him constantly, and as he neared the date for his long "journey" (a metaphor for death), he worried he might never finish his greatest work—a painting of a tree. When it came time for his departure, the artist looked at his painting, and as he feared, saw an unfinished work— nothing but a small leaf and a few details. The majority of the painting he hoped would someday happen never did.

We all can relate to such regret, the pain of leaving some projects undone, fearing we will never return to them. But there is an interesting twist at the end of Tolkien's story. When Niggle completes his journey and enters the afterlife, he sees something he can't believe. Sitting there, in all the glory he imagined, is the tree he never finished.[2]

The work that was not completed in this life was finished in the next.

Many of us fear what Hemingway feared—that we will die with important work still left in us. "We all die unfinished symphonies," a friend told me one morning over breakfast. He was telling me about his dad who, on his deathbed, made a halfhearted attempt to repent for a lifetime of abuse. It wasn't enough for my friend, nor should it have been, but he realized in that moment that he had to let it go anyway. He had to be okay with a lack of resolution, at least in this life. Niggle learned the same thing.

When it comes to your work, there will be things you won't accomplish. This is the work of an artist who bravely steps into their field with bold aspirations, while recognizing the work will never be finished. To paraphrase Leonardo da Vinci, we can never complete the task. We only abandon it.[3] The challenge for any artist—and we are all creating something on the canvas of our lives—is to do our work well while letting go of the result. If we don't do this, we may very well drive ourselves and those around us crazy. And that's the real tragedy—not that we leave this world with work unfinished, but that the work robs us of the life we could have lived. The right choice isn't to retire, to simply settle in and invite death. It's to work hard and passionately, but acknowledge the limitations of what one life is capable of.

The Message of Your Deathbed

Albert Einstein, on his deathbed, asked for his glasses so he could continue working on a project he believed would be his greatest work of all. He was not interested in mere phenomena anymore. He wanted, as he put it, "to know God's thoughts."[4] Everything else was details.

This "theory of everything," as it came to be known, was based on Einstein's belief that physics was an "expression of the divine." He believed there was an explanation for everything, that God did not create chaos but order. He spent thirty years on this project, working on it until the very last day of his life.[5]

What we learn from Einstein and Hemingway is that a healthy fear of death drives a person to continue creating until the very end, but with that fear must come the acceptance that even your life's work will, in some ways, remain unfinished. Why is this, and what do we do with such a humbling reality?

Perhaps one of the proudest achievements in my life is that I was a part of the very first honor code at my college. Founded in 1843, Illinois College had never had an official honor code, a formal document of ethics and academic performance. Such documents were popular in most Ivy League schools, but our small liberal arts school lacked one.

After a professor proposed the idea to the student body government, I realized why our school had never had an honor code. It wasn't for lack of trying. A faculty member gave me a list of students who had attempted to initiate the very thing I was in charge of, and I followed up with each of them. One was a woman who had tried to create a student honor code more than a decade before. E-mailing her, I asked for context, and she told me that it never happened because there was just too much red tape. To me, that sounded like a dare.

For the next year and a half, my friend Dan and I endeavored to do what this young woman didn't, and perhaps couldn't, do. Little did I know how right she was. After drafting dozens of versions of the document, constantly having to change things to appease students, faculty, and staff, I was ready to give up. There was no way to please everyone, and without being able to do that, I was confident we wouldn't be able to garner enough support to pass the document.

Still, we tried: we lobbied the student body, wrote articles in the school newspaper, and met with any professor or administrator who would listen. And on the last day of classes, during our senior year, we submitted our proposal to the faculty for a vote. If there was a majority vote, the honor code would be instituted.

Waiting outside the lecture hall after delivering an impassioned speech about why we needed such a document, I tried to listen to what the results of the vote were. A minute later, the meeting was adjourned, and a hundred professors exited the hall. As one economics professor who had been a proponent of the code passed me, he turned around and not so discreetly winked at me.

I sighed. We had done it.

But the work was far from over. All we had done was take a theory and make it official; now the code had to be enacted. Committees would have to be formed and processes would have to be tested. I had no choice but to pass the baton on to another student, a sophomore named Josh who was passionate about our school and respecting the honorable tradition on which it was founded. I may have been one of the champions for the honor code, but Josh and his classmates completed the task.

—✺—

Recently, I reconnected with Ed Cathey. He was working at another nearby rescue mission as the board director. When we caught up

on the phone, he told me he was sleeping less than ever before—
a few hours a night—and that he missed his wife. She died long
before I ever met Ed. He had to be well into his eighties by now,
and it would have been more than a decade since her death.

He told me he was looking forward to "going home," to dying.
He wasn't sad about this; he was excited to soon be reunited with
his wife. At the same time, he wasn't idly sitting by, waiting for
death to come. Ed was as active as ever, which was what I would
have expected. I asked him what he was most proud of. His answer
surprised me, but it shouldn't have.

Did Ed talk about his years of service at Vanderbilt Hospital?
Did he mention his experiences of singing in concert halls and
leading world-famous choirs? No, he mentioned none of that.
What he told me was story after story of the homeless men whom
he called "son," men he had the privilege of watching graduate
from the rehabilitation program and go on to live healthy lives.
This was his legacy, and it happened in the two decades of his life
after he retired.

Ed answered a call on his life that surprised him. He never
would have imagined himself working at a homeless shelter after
retiring, but when he saw the need, it just made sense. After the
death of his wife, he was heartbroken. So he focused his free time
on serving the less fortunate, a way of turning tragedy into triumph, as Jody Noland had done. His friend introduced him to the
opportunity at the mission in a brief apprenticeship of sorts. And
like Ginny Phang, he was initially uncomfortable with the work,
but the more he did it, the better it fit.

Deciding to work at the mission was one of the most significant pivots of Ed's life, resulting in a legacy of hundreds, if not thousands, of lives changed. But all that is not to disregard the years he spent as a physical therapist and singer, as a dedicated husband and loyal church member. Like Jody Maberry, Ed's calling was not just one thing; it was his whole life—a portfolio with immeasurable ripple effects.

Yes, we all die unfinished symphonies, and the work is never complete. But if you hear the call to make your life about more than you and what you can contribute, you will have peace, not anxiety, when facing mortality. You will realize, as we all do, that you do not have enough resources to complete what you were called to do. Coming to the edge of the Promised Land, you will lack the strength to enter in. The project or company you spent your life trying to get off the ground will need even more management and even more funding to go to the next level. And your time will be finished, even though the work of a calling never ends.

At that point, you can either abandon the work, giving up in despair, or find a way to pass it on. You can do this by building a team, as Ben and Kristy Carlson did, or creating an organization that multiplies your influence. You can plan a better future for your loved ones, as Sam from Uganda did. When we share our life's work, when we accept that we are not done until we're dead, we not only realize our own potential but we also help others do the same. Because in the end, success isn't so much what you do with your life; it's what you leave behind. Which may be what a calling is all about: leaving a legacy that matters.

Dear Reader,

Thank you for joining me through this journey of vocation. My hope is that by now these stories have inspired and encouraged you to find your own calling and that you are already on your way. I'd love for you to visit artofworkbook.com and share your story there, as well as use the resources available. You can also contact me at Goinswriter.com.

Thanks again,

Jeff Goins

#artofworkbook

Acknowledgments

Many thanks to my endlessly patient wife, Ashley, who is my favorite editor ever. She caught so many mistakes in this book that would've made you put the book down before ever getting to this point. And to my little guy, Aiden—thanks, buddy, for being a trouper while I disappeared for a few nights and weekends to finish this thing.

To Joel Miller for acquiring this book and for the numerous nights of talking me off ledges, I am so very appreciative. (You really should go into therapy, Joel. You're quite good at it.) Thanks to Michael Hyatt for introducing us, and to Brian Hampton, Chad Cannon, Katherine Rowley, Belinda Bass, Katy Boatman, Emily Lineberger, and the rest of the team at Nelson Books for their help in completing this work.

My gratitude goes out to my agent, Mark Oestreicher, for doing agent-y things and then some—like actually coming up with the name of the book. Thanks, Marko. Your mentorship has been invaluable in my own process of discovering my calling. I also can't write a book about calling without mentioning Paul Martin, who was the first person to get me to call myself a writer.

Thanks to Christine Niles for helping me edit multiple versions of this book and tracking down all those pesky citations I tend to forget. And to Marion Roach Smith, who helped yet another book of mine cross the finish line, I am grateful. And of course, I cannot forget the My 500 Words Community for all their critiques and encouragement throughout this process. To Jamie Hess for managing the chaos that is my life, thank you. I couldn't do any of this without you!

And to everyone who contributed their stories to this book, thank you! This was such a fun but daunting project, and your experiences really brought it to life.

Thanks to my dad and mom, Keith and Robin Goins, for encouraging me to do my best, but to never try to be someone I was not. And to my in-laws for their constant support: Pam, Pat, Ahron, and Kathy. Thanks, you guys!

Lastly, I thank God for his grace and mercy, for giving me the words to say when I had none, and to you, dear reader, for taking the time to finish this book. It means so much to me, and I hope it has been helpful to you.

Appendix

Your First Steps Down the Path

The seven characteristics of a calling—awareness, apprenticeship, practice, discovery, profession, mastery, and legacy—are not a formula. They are a description of the path you are already on. My hope in sharing them is that you now have a vocabulary with which to explain your vocation as well as a better understanding of what it might be. But what about the next steps to take? What if you now realize you do, in fact, have a calling, and you don't want to waste another minute? Is there a process that can get you started? A series of steps to follow?

So far, we have seen how a calling is both mysterious and practical. In the first part of the book, we explored the ways you prepare for a calling. In the second part, we looked at how people who found their callings took action. In the third part, we saw how a calling is something that needs to be shared with other people. Now I want to offer some practical takeaways and challenges.

The Seven Stages and Accompanying Lessons (Chapter Summary)

1. Awareness: Before you can tell your life what you want to do with it, you must listen to what it wants to do with you.

2. Apprenticeship: Every story of success is a story of community. Although mentors are hard to come by, accidental apprenticeships are everywhere. Your life is preparing you for what's to come.

3. Practice: Real practice hurts. It takes not only time but intentional effort. But some things do come naturally. Be open to learning new skills, and watch for sparks of inspiration to guide you.

4. Discovery: Don't take the leap; build a bridge. You never "just know" what you're supposed to do with your life. Discovery happens in stages.

5. Profession: Failure is your best friend. Don't push through obstacles; pivot around them. Let every mistake and rejection teach you something. Before a season of success, there often comes a season of failure.

6. Mastery: A calling is not just one thing. It's a few things, a portfolio that isn't just your job but the life you live.

7. Legacy: Your calling is not just what you do; it's the person you become—and the legacy you leave.

Seven Signs You've Found Your Calling

1. It's familiar. You find your calling not just by looking forward to what you will do but also by looking back at what you've done.
2. It's something other people see in you. Sometimes our vocations are most obvious to those who know us best.
3. It's challenging. It must be difficult enough that not anyone can do it.
4. It requires faith. It cannot be something so obvious that you can easily explain it. It must be mysterious.
5. It takes time. You have to fail your way in the right direction before you find it.
6. It's more than just one thing. And it integrates well with the rest of your life, not competing with but complementing your top priorities.
7. It's bigger than you. The task must be so large that without a team of people, you cannot complete it on your own.

Next-Step Exercises

Here are seven exercises that will help you get moving in the right direction.

Exercise 1: Create a "listen to your life" timeline. Draw a horizontal line on a piece of paper and use it to plot out the significant events in your life. Look for trends, patterns, and significant moments. Have you always played basketball? As a child, were you fascinated with technology? Was there something unique about you that baffled even your parents? Write it all down, then spend at least thirty minutes reflecting on what all this might mean. Practice this every day until your calling comes into focus. At the same time, reach out to a handful of friends or family members and ask them to describe something that you do better than anyone they know. Sometimes we tend to overlook our greatest assets. Use the timeline and the wisdom of loved ones to help you see a direction you might be missing. (For more on this process, visit artofworkbook.com/listen.)

Exercise 2: Design your own apprenticeship. Don't go in search of a mentor; instead, identify the mentors that are already around you. Who could you ask to meet for coffee or lunch? Make a list of these people and reach out to them. Prepare ahead of time, ask questions, and take notes. Afterward, follow up with a thank-you note, sharing specifically what you learned and how you'd like to do it again. Start meeting regularly with those who reciprocate and let the relationship progress organically. (For more on finding a mentor, visit artofworkbook.com/apprentice.)

Exercise 3: Practice in the margins. Instead of preparing to take some giant leap, start working on your calling today. Don't overcommit. Begin with thirty minutes a day and increase the frequency from there. Make a list of activities you can do to the point of exhaustion and start pushing yourself in them, spending more time on the areas where you have the greatest passion and skill. Pay attention to how you grow or don't grow, and see what that tells you about your calling. (For more on the science of skill acquisition, visit artofworkbook.com/practice.)

Exercise 4: Look for pivot points. Go back to the line you drew in Exercise 1 and mark your greatest moments of failure. When did you try something and it didn't work? Were you rejected by someone or fired from a job? What did you do afterward? Identify the times when you faced an obstacle that forced you in a different direction. What did that tell you about yourself? Now make a list of upcoming pivot points, changes you need to make to create room for your calling. Do you need to quit your job? Move to a new city? Stop writing marketing copy so you can work on that novel? You don't have to know how to make the change; just make the list. Clarity will come with action. (For more on pivoting, visit artofworkbook.com/pivot.)

Exercise 5: Identify discovery moments. Was there a time when something was unclear to you but obvious to someone else? Write about this or share it with a friend. What do others see in you that you don't see in yourself? As an extended exercise, try e-mailing five people who know you well and ask them to describe you. You might be surprised to see what you learn about yourself. (For more on the discovery process and when to take the leap, visit artofworkbook.com/leap.)

Exercise 6: Plan your portfolio. Instead of planning out your ideal week, focus instead on the next year. You have 365 days. How many do you need to support yourself working? How many days do you now have left to do study work, homework, and gift work? Go through the calendar and start marking dates that you could spend on those activities. If you have a family or significant other, go through this exercise with them. You don't have to set anything in stone yet; it's just a way to get a global view of your year and how you can intentionally move in the direction of your life's work. (For more on how to plan your own portfolio, visit artofworkbook.com/portfolio.)

Exercise 7: Share the work. In chapter 7, we saw how a calling is not just about you. It's something you share with others. Begin by making a list of people you could ask to become a part of your team. These can be people you hire for your business or organization, or it can be more informal like a monthly conference call or regular e-mail update, sharing how you're moving toward your calling. Also, identify as many as three people you want to personally invest in. Don't think of this as a formal mentorship; just start showing up in a few people's lives in hopes of helping them grow. (For more on legacy, visit artofworkbook.com/legacy.)

Questions for Discussion

Introduction

The story of Garrett Rush-Miller illustrates how a calling isn't always something you can plan. How has a negative circumstance in your life in some way led to a positive outcome? Do you think it's true that how we react to events determines who we become?

Chapter 1

The story of Jody Noland shows us how pain can awaken us to our purpose. How have you seen that happen in your own life, as well as in the lives of others? When you look back at your life, is there a common theme you can identify? Are the events of your life speaking to you in some way? How could you respond?

Chapter 2

The story of Ginny Phang shows us how even when we feel alone, there are people there to help guide us. Are there people in your life who showed up at just the right time? Can you look back and see your own accidental apprenticeships? Who are the people in your life influencing you right now?

Chapter 3

The stories of Stephanie Fisher and William Hung show us how we can sometimes practice the wrong things, whereas Martyn Chamberlin's story illustrates how a calling can be something you may not have considered. How have you pursued the wrong thing in life? Have you ever succeeded in something that you weren't passionate about? Was there a time when you tried a new skill only to discover you were naturally gifted at something you didn't know anything about?

Chapter 4

The story of Ben and Kristy Carlson shows how successfully pursuing a dream is less about taking a giant leap and more about building a bridge over time. How can you start building a bridge today that will lead to your calling?

Chapter 5

The story of Matt McWilliams illustrates how failure isn't always an enemy but can be an ally that helps us get closer to our life's work. How has something that initially looked like failure to you been the very thing you needed to succeed? What's something you feel like you're failing at right now? What might that be telling you about your calling?

Chapter 6

The story of Jody Maberry shows how a calling isn't a job so much as it is a portfolio of work that you create. What would your ideal portfolio look like? Of the five different types of work Charles Handy shares, which have you overlooked?

Chapter 7

The fictional account of Mr. Holland helps us see how the difference we make can sometimes be taken for granted. What is an example of a time when you were focused on a task when you should have been focusing more on relationships? If you were to have your own Mr. Holland moment, who would you want to be there to celebrate you?

Conclusion

Ed Cathey's story is an illustration of how one man made a difference by investing in others. How could you be more intentional about sharing your calling with others? What is the work that you will start but need others to finish? Who can help you, and whom can you help?

For more study materials, visit artofworkbook.com/guides.

Notes

Introduction

1. "Rush-Miller Foundation," Rush-Miller Foundation, accessed August 1, 2014, http://rushmillerfoundation.org/.
2. Patrice O'Shaughnessy, "Profiles: One Bike at a Time," Nursingcenter.com, accessed August 1, 2014, http://www.nursingcenter.com/lnc/JournalArticle?Article_ID=756067.
3. "Rush-Miller Foundation."
4. Matt King, Team King, accessed August 1, 2014, http://thekinglink.com/.
5. Loretta Sword, "Blindness Poses No Barrier to Determined Family," Cheyenne Mountain Triathlon, June 24, 2001, accessed August 1, 2014, http://rushmillerfoundation.org/images/Phot Alb/Cheyenne2001/Chey2001.htm.
6. Eric Miller and Garrett Rush-Miller, telephone interview by author, February 18, 2014. All direct quotes come from our interview unless otherwise noted. Previous sources were used to fill in backstory, and then reconfirmed with both Eric and Garrett.

Chapter 1

1. Jody Noland, *Leave Nothing Unsaid* (2007), http://leavenothingunsaid.com. Any direct quotes from Jody not

attributed to the phone interview come from her self-published workbook, which can be found and purchased on her website.

2. Jody Noland, telephone interview by author, February 20, 2014.
3. Jim Cash, Jack Epps Jr., and AJ Carothers, *The Secret of My Success*, directed by Herbert Ross (Universal City, CA: Universal Pictures, 1987), DVD.
4. Susan Adams, "Unhappy Employees Outnumber Happy Ones by Two to One Worldwide," Forbes.com, October 10, 2013, accessed July 30, 2014, http://www.forbes.com/sites/susanadams/2013/10/10/unhappy-employees-outnumber-happy-ones-by-two-to-one-worldwide/.
5. Viktor E. Frankl, *Man's Search for Meaning* (Boston: Beacon Press, 2006).
6. Ibid.
7. Brennan Manning, *Ruthless Trust: The Ragamuffin's Path to God* (San Francisco: HarperSanFrancisco, 2000).
8. Frederick Buechner, *Now and Then: A Memoir of Vocation* (Cambridge, MA: Harper & Row, 1983).
9. Parker J. Palmer, *Let Your Life Speak: Listening for the Voice of Vocation* (San Francisco: Jossey-Bass, 2000).
10. Bob Thomas, *Walt Disney: An American Original* (New York: Simon and Schuster, 1976), 39.

Chapter 2

1. Ginny Phang, online interview by author, January 22, 2014.
2. John Donne, "Meditation XVII," *Wikisource*, accessed August 1, 2014, http://en.wikisource.org/wiki/Meditation_XVII.
3. Paulo Coelho, *The Alchemist* (New York: HarperCollins, 2007).
4. Margot Adler, "Apprenticeship, Illumination in a Modern-Day Atelier," *Weekend Edition*, NPR, April 12, 2008.
5. Karin Lipson, "A Medieval Skill Is Nurtured in Gold-Leaf Splendor," NYTimes.com, January 1, 2011, http://www.nytimes.com/2011/01/02/nyregion/02artsli.html?_r=0.
6. Adler, "Apprenticeship, Illumination."

7. Ibid.

8. Ibid.

9. Eric Westervelt, "The Secret to Germany's Low Youth Unemployment," NPR, April 4, 2012, http://www.npr.org/2012 /04/04/149927290/the-secret-to-germanys-low-youth -unemployment.

10. Walter Isaacson, *Steve Jobs* (New York: Simon & Schuster, 2011).

11. Phang, interview.

12. John Burroughs, BrainyQuote, accessed August 1, 2014, http:// www.brainyquote.com/quotes/quotes/j/johnburrou119899 .html.

13. Phang, interview.

Chapter 3

1. Dave Emke, "Chasing Her Dream," *Post-Journal*, February 4, 2010, accessed August 1, 2014, http://www.post-journal.com/ page/content.detail/id/550489/Chasing-Her-Dream.html?nav =5018.

2. "American Idol Reject Stephanie Fisher," YouTube video, 2:53, posted by "Give Peace a Chance," February 3, 2010, accessed August 1, 2014, https://www.youtube.com/watch?v=MtlEG MbDdlw.

3. Ibid.

4. "Seven 'American Idol' Rejects Who Made It Big," Toofab, January 16, 2013, accessed August 1, 2014, http://www.toofab. com/2013/01/16/seven-american-idol-rejects-who-made-it-big -naya-rivera-amber-riley-colbie-caillat-hillary-scott. See also "Colbie Caillat Music - All about Colbie, Music, Pictures & Info," Colbie Caillat Music, accessed August 1, 2014, http:// www.colbiecaillatmusic.com/.

5. Geoffrey Colvin, *Talent Is Overrated: What Really Separates World-Class Performers from Everybody Else* (New York: Penguin, 2008).

6. Geoffrey Colvin, " Why Talent Is Overrated," *Fortune Magazine*,

October 21, 2008, accessed August 1, 2014, archive.fortune.com
/2008/10/21/magazines/fortune/talent_colvin.fortune/index.htm.

7. "Seven 'American Idol' Rejects Who Made It Big."

8. Carol S. Dweck, *Mindset: The New Psychology of Success* (New York: Random House, 2006).

9. Ibid.

10. K. Anders Ericsson, Ralf Th. Krampe, and Clemens Tesch-Römer, "The Role of Deliberate Practice in the Acquisition of Expert Performance," *Psychological Review* (100, no. 3 1993): 363–406.

11. Daniel Coyle, *The Talent Code: Greatness Isn't Born. It's Grown. Here's How* (New York: Random House, 2009).

12. Ibid.

13. Ericsson, Krampe, and Tesch-Römer, "The Role of Deliberate Practice."

14. Ibid.

15. Ibid.

16. Kim Wilson, Kelly Candaele, Lowell Ganz, and Babaloo Mandel, *A League of Their Own*, directed by Penny Marshall (United States: Sony Pictures Home Entertainment, 1992), DVD.

17. Ericsson, Krampe, and Tesch-Römer, "The Role of Deliberate Practice."

18. Martyn Chamberlin, phone interview by author, December 13, 2013.

19. David J. Epstein, *The Sports Gene: Inside the Science of Extraordinary Athletic Performance* (New York: Penguin, 2013).

20. Daniel Coyle, online interview by author, February 19, 2014.

21. James C. Collins and Morten T. Hansen, *Great by Choice: Uncertainty, Chaos, and Luck: Why Some Thrive Despite Them All* (New York: HarperCollins, 2011).

22. Ericsson, Krampe, and Tesch-Römer, "The Role of Deliberate Practice."

23. "William Hung American Idol Audition - SHE BANGS!" YouTube video, 1:40, posted by "Ben Lee," August 13, 2007, accessed August 1, 2014, https://www.youtube.com/watch?v=2Qkas9mlMgE.

24. *Wikipedia*, s.v. "William Hung," last modified April 2014, http://en.wikipedia.org/wiki/William_Hung.
25. "William Hung interview," YouTube video, 2:42, posted by "StevenWard," March 18, 2008, https://www.youtube.com/watc h?v=qOcwvR8WWoo&feature=player_embedded.
26. Daniel Kohn, "William Hung Speaks, Fresh off Being Crowned the Greatest Musician of All Time, in Any Genre," *LA Weekly*, January 16, 2012, http://www.laweekly.com/ westcoastsound/2012/01/16/william-hung-speaks-fresh-off -being-crowned-the-greatest-musician-of-all-time-in-any-genre.
27. "William Hung interview," YouTube video.
28. Kohn, "William Hung Speaks."
29. "William Hung - She Bangs Speech - Toastmasters - Founders District," YouTube video, 4:39, posted by "Chris David," September 26, 2013, https://www.youtube.com/watch?v =FQctx-n-FTA.
30. Ibid.

Additional Sources:

Samantha Grossman, "American Idol's William Hung: Where Is He Now?" Time.com, January 19, 2012, accessed August 1, 2014, http://newsfeed.time.com/2012/01/19/american-idols -william-hung-where-is-he-now/.
Mireya Navarro, "Missing: Asian-American Pop Stars," NYTimes.com, March 4, 2007, http://www.nytimes.com/2007 /03/04/world/americas/04iht-singer.4787848.html.
Corey Moss, "William Hung's Sales Figures Are Nothing to Laugh At," MTV.com, April 12, 2004, http://www.mtv.com/news/ articles/1486330/william-hung-cd-actually-selling-well.jhtml.

Chapter 4

1. Ben and Kristy Carlson, e-mail interview by author, January 14, 2014.
2. Long Miles Coffee Project, accessed August 2, 2014, http:// www.longmilescoffeeproject.com/.

3. Frederick Buechner, *Now and Then: A Memoir of Vocation* (Cambridge, MA: Harper & Row, 1983).
4. 1 Samuel 1–3, *The Holy Bible: New International Version* (Grand Rapids: Zondervan Bible Publishers, 1978).
5. Ginny Phang, online interview by author, January 22, 2014.
6. "Burundi: Belgian Colonial Rule (1916–1962)," EISA (Electoral Institute for Sustainable Democracy in Africa), April 2010, http://eisa.org.za/WEP/buroverview3.htm.
7. Michael B. Sauter, Alexander E. M. Hess, and Samuel Weigley, "The 10 Poorest Countries in the World," Fox Business, September 14, 2012, http://www.foxbusiness.com /markets/2012/09/14/10-poorest-countries-in-world/.
8. Brent Swails and Oliver Joy, "Burundi's Coffee Culture 'the Difference Between Food and Hunger,'" CNN, November 19, 2013, http://edition.cnn.com/2013/11/19/business/burundis -coffee-culture.
9. Sauter, Hess, and Weigley, "The 10 Poorest Countries in the World."
10. Johnstone S. Oketch and Tara Polzer, "Conflict and Coffee in Burundi," *Scarcity and Surfeit*, September 19, 2013, http://www .issafrica.org/pubs/Books/ScarcitySurfeit/Chapter3.pdf, 84–156.
11. Thompson Owen and Christopher Schooley, "Rwanda + Burundi Fundamentals," Coffeeshrub.com, accessed August 1, 2014, http://www.coffeeshrub.com/shrub/content/rwanda -burundi-fundamentals.
12. Bryan Allain, online interview by author, August 4, 2014.
13. Carlson, interview.

Chapter 5

1. Matt McWilliams, online interview by author, February 20, 2014.
2. Nicholas Carlson, "Inside Groupon: The Truth About the World's Most Controversial Company," Business Insider, October 31, 2011, http://www.businessinsider.com/inside

-groupon-the-truth-about-the-worlds-most-controversial-company-2011-10.

3. Ibid.
4. Alistair Barr and Clare Baldwin, "Groupon IPO: Company Raises $700 Million, Valued at $12.8 Billion," Huffington Post, November 4, 2011, http://www.huffingtonpost.com/2011/11/04/groupon-ipo-biggest-since-google_n_1075374.html.
5. Robert Greene, *Mastery* (New York: Penguin, 2012).
6. Ira Stoll, *Samuel Adams: A Life* (New York: Simon & Schuster, 2008).
7. Ibid.
8. Ibid.
9. Brennan Manning, *Ruthless Trust: The Ragamuffin's Path to God* (San Francisco: HarperSanFrancisco, 2000).
10. Pedro Calderón de la Barca, *Life Is a Dream: La Vida Es Sueño* (Public Domain, 1635).
11. Eric Metaxas, *Bonhoeffer: Pastor, Martyr, Prophet, Spy: A Righteous Gentile vs. the Third Reich* (Nashville: Thomas Nelson, 2010), 337.
12. Eberhard Bethge, *Dietrich Bonhoeffer: Eine Biographie* (Minneapolis: Fortress Press, 2000), 736.
13. Metaxas, *Bonhoeffer*, 530–532.
14. Ibid., 123–24.

Chapter 6

1. Jody Maberry, online interview by author, May 12, 2014.
2. Thomas Fisher, "The Contingent Workforce and Public Decision Making," *Public Sector Digest*, March 2012: 46–48. Several articles and other publications have made similar predictions: Jeff Wald, "How an Exploding Freelance Economy Will Drive Change in 2014," Forbes.com, November 25, 2013, http://www.forbes.com/sites/groupthink/2013/11/25/how-an-exploding-freelance-economy-will-drive-change-in-2014/; Elaine Pofeldt, "What You'll Need to Know to Be the Boss in 2020,"

Forbes.com, April 3, 2012, http://www.forbes.com/sites/
elainepofeldt/2012/04/03/what-youll-need-to-know-to-be-the
-boss-in-2020; Ryan Kim, "By 2020, Independent Workers Will
Be the Majority," Gigaom, December 8, 2011, http://gigaom.com
/2011/12/08/mbo-partners-network-2011.

3. Charles B. Handy, *The Age of Unreason* (Boston: Harvard
Business School Press, 1989).

5. Hara Estroff Marano, "The Power of Play," *Psychology Today*,
January 28, 2013, http://www.psychologytoday.com/articles
/199907/the-power-play.

6. Natalie Cooper, "Lessons in Leadership, Work and Wellbeing
05/09/2013," changeboard.com, May 9, 2013, http://www.
changeboard.com/content/4237/career-development/personal
-branding/lessons-in-leadership-work-and-wellbeing/.

7. Peter M. Senge, *The Fifth Discipline: The Art & Practice of the
Learning Organization* (New York: Doubleday/Currency, 1990).

8. Dorothy Sayers, "Why Work?" accessed August 2, 2014, http://
www.faith-at-work.net/Docs/WhyWork.pdf.

9. Ibid.

10. Mihaly Csikszentmihalyi, *Flow: The Psychology of Optimal
Experience* (New York: Harper & Row, 1990).

11. Ibid.

12. Maberry, interview.

13. Jody Maberry, "Finding My Calling," e-mail message to author,
January 6, 2014.

Chapter 7

1. Patrick Sheane Duncan, *Mr. Holland's Opus*, directed
by Stephen Herek (Burbank, CA: Buena Vista Home
Entertainment, 1999), DVD.

2. Ibid.

3. John Lennon, "Beautiful Boy (Darling Boy)," *Double Fantasy*,
Geffen Records, April 11, 1981.

4. May Sarton, *Collected Poems, 1930–1993* (New York: W. W.
Norton, 1993).

5. Ezra Pound, *Poems and Translations* (New York: Literary Classics of the United States, 2003).

6. Gloria Stronks, "Where Does the World Need Me?" Cardus, December 27, 2013, http://www.cardus.ca/comment/article /4124/where-does-the-world-need-me/.

7. Oliver Wendell Holmes, *The Writings of Oliver Wendell Holmes: The Poetical Works* (Boston: Riverside Press, 1891), 247.

8. Mike Rich, *Finding Forrester*, directed by Gus Van Sant (Culver City, CA: Columbia TriStar Home Video, 2000), DVD.

9. Stephen King, *On Writing: A Memoir of the Craft* (New York: Scribner, 2000).

10. Ibid.

11. Jennifer Crittenden, "And Maggie Makes Three," *The Simpsons*, season 6, episode 13, directed by Swinton Scott, aired January 22, 1995.

Conclusion

1. A. E. Hotchner, *Papa Hemingway: A Personal Memoir* (New York: Random House, 1966).

2. J. R. R. Tolkien, *Tree and Leaf* (Boston: Houghton Mifflin, 1965).

3. Leonardo da Vinci quote, BrainyQuote, accessed August 2, 2014, http://www.brainyquote.com/quotes/quotes/l/leonardoda 380290.html.

4. "Einstein's Unfinished Symphony," BBC, accessed September 15, 2014, http://www.bbc.co.uk/sn/tvradio/programmes/horizon /einstein_symphony_prog_summary.shtml.

5. Ibid.

About the Author

J eff Goins is a full-time writer who lives just outside of Nashville, Tennessee, with his wife, son, and border collie. He has authored three other books: *The In-Between*, *Wrecked*, and *You Are a Writer*. He spent a year after college traveling around the United States with a band, and they hit it big in Taiwan. His website, Goinswriter.com, has been visited by more than four million people from all over the world. Connect with him on Twitter (@jeffgoins), visit his website to say hi, or stop by for some homemade guacamole the next time you're in town. You can also get more free resources at artofworkbook.com.

Goinswriter.com

#artofworkbook